Unveiling
THE Prophet

T0163336

Tom K. Smith, the 1972 Veiled Prophet, attempting to restore his hat and veil, December 22, 1972. (Photo courtesy of the *St. Louis Post-Dispatch*)

Unveiling ᴛʜᴇ Prophet

The Misadventures of
a Reluctant Debutante

Lucy Ferriss

University of Missouri Press
Columbia and London

Library of Congress Cataloging-in-Publication Data

Ferriss, Lucy, 1954–
    Unveiling the prophet : the misadventures of a reluctant debutante /
Lucy Ferriss.
        p. cm.
    ISBN-13: 978-0-8262-1601-4 (alk. paper)
    ISBN-10: 0-8262-1601-3 (alk. paper)
    1. Ferriss, Lucy, 1954–   —Homes and haunts—Missouri—Saint Louis.
2. Authors, American—Homes and haunts—Missouri—Saint Louis.
3. Ferriss, Lucy, 1954–   —Childhood and youth. 4. Authors, American
—20th century—Biography. 5. Saint Louis (Mo.)—Social life and
customs. 6. Veiled Prophets of Saint Louis (Order : Mo.) 7. Debutante balls—Missouri—Saint Louis.   I. Title.
    PS3556.E754Z477 2005
    813'.54—dc22
                                                          2005015194

♾™ This paper meets the requirements of the
American National Standard for Permanence of Paper
for Printed Library Materials, Z39.48, 1984.

Designer: Stephanie Foley
Typesetter: Foley Design
Printer and binder: Thomson-Shore, Inc.
Typefaces: Bembo and Meridien

⌘   ⌘   ⌘

Publication of this book has been assisted by the
William Peden Memorial Fund

Contents

The mystic pageant temperament pervades all St. Louis. It is lacking in most other cities of approximate latitude. It does not exist to any degree on the Atlantic coast or on the Great Lakes. It is unknown beyond the Rocky Mountains. But here, in the heart of the country, with the most thoroughly composite population, the most typical Americans, the Veiled Prophet is at home.

— Walter B. Stevens, *St. Louis, the Fourth City,* 1764-1909

Miss Scott . . . is being held at police headquarters on a previous charge of nonpayment of parking fines. Veiled Prophet officers would not press any charges against her, police said.

— *St. Louis Post-Dispatch,* December 23, 1972

There is no honor more dear to the daughters of St. Louis than to be chosen as Consort of his mysterious highness, and none more eagerly sought. . . . For, while his majesty is fickleness itself, with a new queen each year, his sense of grace and charm seems most intuitive. Surely, the Prophet, with his unfailing contemplation of loveliness, has added the sweet tyranny of beauty as a perpetual benediction to his gentle rule over his Court of Love and Beauty.

— *His Mysterious Majesty the Veiled Prophet's Golden Jubilee,* 1928

This Ku Klux Klan gathering of wealthy fat cats [is] auctioning off their daughters to the highest bidder. . . while Black and powerless people burn.

— ACTION, open letter, 1972

Acknowledgments

I am grateful to those who were willing to revisit their roles in the 1972 Veiled Prophet Ball: Percy Green, Joan Dames, Mary Ann Fitzgerald, Laura Rand Orthwein (Laura X), Margaret Phillips, Jane Sauer, and Gena Scott. Many thanks to Marie and John Brauer for their hospitality. Dr. Thomas Spencer was generous with his unique understanding of the history of the Veiled Prophet and St. Louis. The librarians at the Mercantile Library in St. Louis, the Missouri Historical Society, and the interlibrary loan departments of Hamilton College and Trinity College helped with resources and photo retrieval. Carolyn Mascaro of the Hamilton College English Department patiently transcribed interview tapes. Thanks also to my siblings, Dan Ferriss and Juliet Woulfe, and my cousin Donald Harris, for jogging my memory, providing information, and reading drafts. Fred Pfeil, Irene Papoulis, Dori Katz, Robert Peltier, Liz Libbey, Christine McMorris, Eric Goodman, and Thalia Selz read every word and kept this book alive in manuscript. Thanks to Jeffery Hammond for the invitation photographs. Clair Willcox and Susan King at the University of Missouri Press are my editing heroes. The spirit of my parents, Ann and Franklin Ferriss, pervades these pages despite their understandable qualms about the subject, and I dedicate this book to their memory. A few unimportant names in this text have been changed to preserve their privacy. All errors of fact are the sole responsibility of the author.

Unveiling
THE Prophet

Prologue

1965

Seventh grade. We are free to walk the halls, somewhat less free to choose our destinations. One heads for Art and another for French; one for Math-A with Miss Sachar, another for B-1 (dummies) with Mr. Birdwell. Dim and full of wood, the halls echo our shouts in a shrill, minor key. All in skirts, all pale, and all girls. Most of the teachers are girls, too, whom we despise—unless they are very young—for having to work. Our mothers are women, and they don't work. We giggle over the few male teachers, for whom we also preen ourselves. Drably elegant curtains hang along the walls of the refectory, patched with zigzag lines of stitching at which we pick, pick, pick as we wait our turn in the lunch line. The whey-faced ladies who dish out our food are not really women at all but animated yeast rolls, like the Pillsbury Dough Boy. Cleaning the school building, after we have left the hockey fields and study halls, are dark shadow men. You can look right through them.

Our seventh-grade teacher, Beatrice Striker—she of the high gray bun and aristocratic nose, known through the grades as Busybee—informs us that the Ku Klux Klan has been unfairly criticized: were it not for these brave, kindly men and women in the South, she says, many children now would be going without shoes. We are to picture the Ku Klux Klan as a sort of Junior League in white sheets. Our main project this year is to make our own marionettes and act out a Shakespeare play. Busybee assigns me the part of Kate in *The Taming of the Shrew* and tells me it is typecasting. We also raise money to buy a pair of sea horses that we install in Busybee's personal aquarium, in the corner of the room. In early October, the sea horses float to the top like fragile treble clefs. Busybee excoriates us: we are the first class to lose its sea horses. She never thought she would live to see the day.

Connie Farnsworth pees in her classroom seat because she is afraid to raise her hand and ask Mrs. Striker to go to the bathroom. This seems to be funny because Connie is expendable. I wonder if her mother teaches in the Lower School. The girls whose mothers teach attend this school free of charge. In seventh grade, you get what you pay for. For months, Connie Farnsworth goes through the halls with girls' teasing remarks wrapped around her neck like barbed wire. Got your diaper pinned, Connie? Why didn't you get Busybee to wipe your seat, Connie? What perfume you wearing, Connie? Going to your mother's class?

I hug my own secret with my books: my mother, too, works. She doesn't work in this school. My mother works at McDonnell Douglas Corporation out on Olive Street Road. I don't know what she does exactly, though she's explained it more than once. Every hour that I'm in school, she's out there. I fear that the school's given me a break in tuition; no one at home will tell me. If the other girls find out any of this, I have only one line of defense: my aunt, Ann Chittenden Ferriss, my father's sister, was Veiled Prophet Queen.

One

The Letter

Oh, where would we be without the classes!
— SAMUEL BUTLER

To an eighteen-year-old girl from St. Louis, Southern California in 1972 was a dazzling place. Palm trees and peyote, saltwater and salt-rimmed margaritas, the jagged eruption of mountain from desert. I claimed to have chosen a college here, as opposed to the more coveted Northeast, because I wanted no more snow. In fact, when applying to schools two years earlier, I had spread out a map of the United States and figured on the place that would be farthest from St. Louis without having to cross an ocean. I wanted no more of what I had grown up with. I wanted to have fun, fun, fun till my daddy took the T-Bird away.

Just before Thanksgiving 1972, I received a letter from St. Louis. This in itself was not unusual; the letters had been flying between Missouri and California, portents of the events of winter. My father, divorced for a year from my mother, would be remarried on December 20. Two days later, I was to be presented at the Veiled Prophet Ball. Five weeks thereafter, I planned to leave school in order to chase a boy to Europe.

Days not consumed by such plans were filled, that fall of my sophomore year, with political activism. Having stolen the election, Nixon was mining Haiphong Harbor. Those of us still in Peace Action on the college campus were organizing marches, writing letters, inviting speakers. The previous year, Jane Fonda had come

3

to our school. A freshman, I had ended up introducing her because I was the only member of Peace Action who sang in the college choir. Ms. Fonda was to speak and show her slides in Bridges Auditorium, which fell under the purview of the music department. Hence I had been summoned as the link between politics and art. I had worn an orange rayon top and hot pants for the occasion; Ms. Fonda had worn a work shirt and jeans. I did not know whether to call her "Jane" or "Ms. Fonda." After she spoke, she stored her tapes in my dorm room so they would not melt in the heat. Together we went to the Peace Rally where she sat in Tom Hayden's lap.

The letter from St. Louis, then, arrived in the midst of plans and changes, and I was not inclined to pay it too much heed. Thus far, at college, I had received St. Louis letters only from my father, mother, and sister, who was still in high school. My brother, like me, was starting his sophomore year, but at a college on the other side of the country. My father's letters were full of admonishments, my mother's full of gossip, and my sister's full of complaint, she being the one left behind amid the detritus of my parents' divorce.

Already, by the fall of 1972, I had begun to tell new friends that I hailed, vaguely, from the Midwest. I did not name the city. I had no idea that they regarded St. Louis the same way they might regard Cleveland or Minneapolis, as an unfamiliar industrial metropolis that might have been mentioned in a song they had heard. I feared they would attach to me what I saw as St. Louis's pathetic attempts to establish legendary status, its economic failure, its faded aristocracy. Only to a few had I admitted that I had a command performance back home, early that coming winter. These were the friends I had taken along with me while I tried on ball gowns.

My mother had sent me one hundred and forty dollars to spend on a dress. This seemed to me an immense sum—a ridiculous waste, according to the manifesto of my compeers, for one evening's adornment. The only acceptable way to spend it was to make the purchase itself a happening, a send-up of the activity we were involved in, as a love-in was a mockery of romantic love, a be-in of socially sanctioned identity. So I invited my new California friends. At the big department stores downtown, I promised them, we could all drink sherry while I tried on ball gowns. We could go from one formal-wear department to the next until we got completely schnockered, and then I would choose something and we'd head down to the beach and smoke weed.

And so we had driven to Westwood, in Kevin Peters's rattling Plymouth—Kevin and Michael Edson and Linda Seligmann and I, and I had felt like the Queen of the Hippies as we sashayed in our ragged bell-bottoms into the formal-wear departments of I. Magnin, of Saks, of Neiman-Marcus. Sure enough, all those attending were given a choice between sherry and coffee. I slipped into the fitting rooms and was brought one billowing cloud of fluff after another. I emerged and pranced. Everyone with me found it hilarious. The saleswomen did not find it hilarious, but I supposed we were educating them, were giving them a peek at the generation that was going to bring down this whole flimsy world of theirs. Now, of course, I realize that they had seen our sort before, had seen through our frivolity to our yearning and also to the cash in our pampered pockets.

But the day was bright in Los Angeles, and the streets wide. If I ever thought these friends of mine were not the true friends I sought, I had only to recall a certain boy studying in Europe who—whether he knew it or not—was waiting for me, was in love with me. We drove with the windows of Kevin's car open, and the radio played Mick Jagger's "You Can't Always Get What You Want." In our fourth department store—my friends' eyes starting to glaze over with the sherry, it was only two in the afternoon and they were not such heavyweights as they claimed—I twirled before them in a confection that roused applause. The long-sleeved top was a clingy purple synthetic knit, scalloped at the neck and wrists and stopping at a natural waist, from which flared a full-length skirt of taffeta cut on the bias, with multicolored candy stripes that swirled like liquid sugar when I moved.

"Far *out*," said Linda Seligmann, whose eyes got smaller when she drank and whose heavy, brown locks came over her eyes to obscure the forehead of acne that embarrassed her.

I took the dress. The saleswoman looked long and hard at my check, then at me, and she made a phone call, but eventually she boxed the delicious thing up while I had a celebratory sherry and we caromed down to the beach.

Underneath my delighted scorn lay both pride and fear. I had found a dress I loved, a dress which almost made me look pretty. But was it the right dress? Would my mother consider the money well spent? So much money! In the ensuing weeks, alone in my dorm room, I had stared at the closed box and bit my nails. It was my own fault that my mother had handed the choice of a dress over to me. The previous summer had seen the usual round of deb parties, and I had spurned her careful homemade efforts at summer gowns, had stomped on her motherly gifts. Now I was supposed to know what I was doing, and I realized beneath my bravado that I had not been paying attention.

And then came the letter from St. Louis.

I had heard of the writer, Percy Green. He had been in the news, a devil figure sent to drive the ruling class of St. Louis mad. Eight years earlier, when the St. Louis Arch was being built, Percy Green had installed himself on a beam 125 feet above the ground, with a sign reading "EQUALITY" on his back, until the construction firm hired by the city agreed to employ black workers. That gesture had been one of the first by Percy's group, ACTION. And although in 1972 I had no idea what the acronym referred to, I had learned from my parents and teachers that Percy Green was to be feared. I understood that his organization was a cell of the Black Panthers, making him a Communist and a terrorist; that the black people who followed him hated whites; that he loved making trouble for no reason. I also knew that my former high-school Latin teacher, Miss Phillips, herself a Communist, was somehow involved with him, making her a member of the Black Panthers.

It was thus with a surge of excitement that I unfolded the letter.

"Dear Lucy Ann," it began, cleverly addressing me by name, "ACTION understands that you hate being part of this up-coming white racist Veiled Prophet Ball as we hate you being forced to participate by your parents."

The letter went on to indict the leaders of the secret Veiled Prophet Society, sponsors of the cotillion for which I had just bought my candy-cane dress. These were the same leaders of major

St. Louis corporations—McDonnell Douglas, Ralston Purina, Budweiser Brewing, Monsanto Chemical, Brown Shoe—who discriminated against Blacks in their hiring practices. They were responsible for the city and state discrimination that trapped so many Black families in the cycle of poverty.

We didn't say "black," yet, in my family. We certainly didn't capitalize it. We still said "Negroes" or "colored people." Sometimes my father said "pickaninnies," and snickered. Very recently, my mother had started saying "the blacks," as if they were a baseball team or a tribe or a class of people like hobbits.

What Percy Green wanted me to do was to renounce my role in this hideous spectacle. I could, he suggested, withdraw my name from the list of debutantes. Or I might keep my name on the list and send my complimentary tickets to him, Percy Green. He and his organization would then present the tickets when they appeared, appropriately dressed, at the door, to be turned away out of racism. The ball was being held in a public space, maintained at taxpayer expense. "As you may already know," the letter went on, "six (6) of the 'maids of honor' have been meeting with us making preparations for the December 22 white V.P. protest demonstration. It's going to be a shocker!"

The writer of the letter begged a reply, "In a humane struggle, Chm. Percy Green."

For several days the letter gathered dust on the small, blond desk in my dorm room. My room was on the first floor of a hacienda-style building, looking out onto the courtyard. When I arrived at school that fall, I had brought with me a kitten, forbidden but tolerated by the authorities. I had named him Socrates, and for the first six weeks of school, sitting on my lap as I studied, he comforted me with his hyperactive purr.

I had drawn a single room, my request. You were allowed to paint your own room any color so long as you used the college's supplies of paint. I chose a rich ivory for the walls, chocolate trim for the molding. Next door lived blond Susan, the only woman I'd met who was skinnier than I. She was so skinny that her gums were receding from her teeth and she had doctor's orders to drink three tall glasses of Nutriment every day. She had a high-pitched giggle and dated a guy named Claude, who stuttered; I envied them their easy love, their maimed comfort with one another. Down the hall in the other direction lived a woman who kept a pet tarantula. Upstairs lived men, but we were beyond rules and curfews, and visitors roamed our hall at all hours. This would have been fine except that I had not wished for the visitors I got—visitors like Nick Peterson, who was the chair of the philosophy department and who gave me the creeps even though he looked like Robert Vaughn in *The Man from U.N.C.L.E.* Visitors like Michael Edson, who stroked his long beard and adjusted his thick glasses and spoke always with a marijuana whine about how fucked up everything was and how I ought to be practicing transcendental meditation and having sex with him.

And then Socrates had died. Suddenly, and most likely from ingesting cleaning fluid left by the staff during the monthly scouring of our rooms. Susan next door passed along an article detailing the relationship between commercial cleaners and cat fatalities. "Sort of like his ancestor and the hemlock," she'd said, with her nervous giggle.

So I read Percy Green's letter over and over, in the loneliness of my cream-and-brown room, my thin Indian cotton bedspread still smelling faintly of incense, the tarantula roaming the hall outside. I smoked Virginia Slims, a habit I was determined to cultivate. Outside my window, bougainvillea and bird-of-paradise filled the courtyard; at its center an old stone fountain cheerfully trickled. Creating my own life had begun to seem a tremendously difficult task, and I had not made a good start.

Finally I pulled out a legal pad. "Dear Percy Green," I began. That was a fair salutation, I thought. He was older than I, so that even if he had addressed me only by my Christian name I shouldn't necessarily respond in kind. It was a bit like the Jane Fonda problem, only easier to solve on paper. I continued:

> You are absolutely right. The Veiled Prophet Ball is nothing but a racist, sexist, imperialist show of power. On the other hand, my father has been shelling out money since I was born so that he could see me walk out on the carpet at Kiel Auditorium, bow to

pay obeisance to the male prerogative, and take my place on the stage. I cannot let him down.

Think about it. Don't you have bigger fish to fry? This is just a stupid party. We are slaughtering people in Southeast Asia. Let this one go. It will fall of its own weight.

Yours in solidarity, etc.

Pleased with myself, I sent the letter off. A day or two later, I got a phone call from my mother. This was unusual. Long distance was expensive and indulgent, reserved for emergencies.

She had heard about a letter, my mother said, that had gone out to all the debs. Had I received such a letter? And had I managed to buy a dress yet?

I was warming, by now, to my task. "I got a great dress," I told her. "You'll love it. I owe you ten bucks back, even."

"Will you need a padded bra?"

"Mother!"

"Sometimes the shape isn't right," she said, trying to be diplomatic, "without a proper bra."

"The shape is great. I brought friends with me. They said I looked pretty in it."

"You are a nice-looking girl," said my mother. "So you didn't get this letter?"

"Sure, I got it," I said. I chewed the end of my Bic. This, too, was part of the creed—we would no longer deny, deny, but would admit, admit. Show them we were unafraid of their strictures.

"Well." She sounded relieved. "Just throw it out."

"I answered it," I said, and told her what I had written.

When she spoke, her voice tight with frustration, my pulse quickened even as I felt a rush of pity. Ninety percent of her effort, my mother had once told me, had been expended upon me. "That was a very poor choice," my mother told me.

Most of my choices, I would have liked to tell her, were poor. Most of them were not yet my own. Guiding my hand in one direction was irony, in the other convention. How a girl like me could make good choices was something I could not yet understand.

Two

The Date

Old enough, now, to change your name.

— CROSBY, STILLS, NASH & YOUNG, 1969

Here are some things I have learned since 1972.

In 1500, the average age of menarche was eighteen. By the age of twenty, most women had borne a child.

In 2005, on average the first egg drops at the age of eleven. The average woman bears her first child at twenty-five.

The "coming-out party" is dubbed by most scholars to be a rite of passage. In the Sudan, they knock out a girl's tooth. Tribal girls, one observer pointed out, "do what is expected of them—and get married." The choice is not really theirs.

The courts at which girls were first presented were drafty, damp places full of people who didn't trust one another. A quick glance at England's royal houses—Wessex, Denmark, Normandy, Atholl, Plantagenet, Blois, Bruce, Lancaster, York, Stuart, Tudor—tells the story of marriage as land acquisition. In Spain, John II crowned his union of Aragon, Valencia, and Catalonia by buying Isabella of Castile for his son Ferdinand. The marriage alliances arranged by Louis XI and Francis I in fifteenth-century France brought a dozen domains together, with the Valois marriage to Anne of Brittany considered the triumph of ruthless diplomacy.

Anthropologists call this practice *endogamy*, a term that sounds to me like a female condition lodged in the fallopian tubes. These marriages, I have learned, were often arranged beforehand. The court presentation was simply a means of showing the world what goods you had managed to sell, or how favored the prince was who had bought them. Only as the notion of measuring a wife's value by way of her uselessness descended downward did presentation to society acquire the gamesmanship quality depicted in Jane Austen's novels, where scheming mothers of girls battle wits with class-conscious fathers of boys to prove the truth that Mrs. Bennett held to be "universally acknowledged, that a single man in possession of a good fortune should be in want of a wife." And only as rank, military service, and the prospect of inheritance began to delay marriage for men did the age at which a girl was presented start to creep upward.

In a Bantu village the period of preparation might last a week. In Regency England, it extended to four, five, six years past the onset of menstruation. When a girl was finally put on the market, the game was all or nothing. Even if you didn't come out of the hut until nineteen, by twenty-one you were nonetheless an old maid. "Three girls," as Jane Austen comments in *Persuasion,* "was an awful legacy for a mother to bequeath."

⌘   ⌘   ⌘

Fortunately, I was only a Maid. Had my father possessed his own father's ambition and drive, he might have continued in private law practice. He might have garnered the reputation and fortune that would have boosted me to the rank of Special Maid, of which there were four. Special Maids had to have two escorts.

But my father had run for the circuit court on the Republican ticket at the age of forty-two, and he had remained on the county bench ever since. By his status was my status determined. Being but a Maid, I needed just one warm, white male date to accompany me to the ball.

I received this news, like Percy Green's letter, in California. A form arrived, along with my complimentary tickets, asking the name and address of my escort. I was stumped.

Dating, I had thought, was obsolete. My few sporadic attempts at it, back in St. Louis, had been markedly unsuccessful. At sixteen, I had asked my brother, Dan, whom I knew to be honest, why it was that I had no success with dating. It was true that we lived in town—in Clayton, that is, the county seat, rather than Ladue, like most of the girls who attended Mary Institute with me. Founded by T. S. Eliot's family to accommodate the daughters of Washington University faculty, Mary Institute catered more by then to the daughters of CEOs, who made their social connections through the St. Louis Country Club—a privilege, I had been made to understand, that my parents had sacrificed in order to have me. So I was handicapped socially, but still. I looked all right, didn't I? And I dressed well? I wasn't stupid, surely, or annoying.

Dan said he would think about this question. A day later, he came to me with his response. "The reason is," he said, as gently as a brother could, "you have no personality."

"He's right," I wrote that night in my diary. "I have plumbed the depths of my soul. And there is no personality in me."

I wore my lack of personality like a badge of pride, the way a person might flaunt a missing limb. My suffering was visible to the world, the girl born without personality.

This had not helped my dating life.

In California, I had discovered, one did not have to date. One hung out. When the chemistry seemed right, one paired off. The Student Health Center aggressively marketed the Pill. Personality seemed as unnecessary as shoes.

There were, to be sure, certain boundaries. For the most part, white hung with white, Chicana with Chicano, black with black. I had tried explaining this setup to my father in St. Louis, the previous Christmas, but he had not been convinced. He had had a warning to deliver, one day when we had lunch near the courthouse, and he was not to be dissuaded from his oracle.

My father was old, as fathers went. Forty-three at my birth, a handsome man, he had started to acquire my grandfather's vulture look, shoulders hunched and nose beaking. His divorce was just barely final, that Christmas, and he pointedly enjoyed the looks he got, old Judge Ferriss squiring a babe around town. We ate at the bar association—white tablecloths, white waiters, black busboys, hushed voices. My father nodded and waved to the other men and confessed that he lost track of their names. "Doesn't matter," he said conspiratorially. "You nod, you smile. You want them to vote for you, that's all. You don't have to know a damn thing about them."

People had been voting for my father as long as I could remember. He'd had to run on a party ticket until 1968. Time and again, he liked to report, he had been the only Republican reelected. Early memories have me standing in the November dark, the proper distance from the polling booth, holding a large cardboard placard sporting my father's pale, somber face with a flag in the background. Once, on our way home from the Episcopal church, he'd spotted a pair of teenage boys tearing up his sign in a vacant lot. He stopped the car to chase them down, clutching his hat to his head as he ran, the living embodiment of the mug on the signboard. To my mortification we had all driven to the boys' house and stood there in our starched clothes while he delivered a tongue-lashing to their small, pasty parents.

No one carded minors at the bar association. I ordered a whiskey sour, my favorite drink and the only mixed cocktail I knew. My father waited until I had sipped and then informed me that my first cousin Susan had gone and involved herself with a black man.

"We don't know how it happened," he said, like a parent accounting for the gun that loaded itself and dropped down from the high shelf into his six-year-old's hands. Susan and her mother, my father reported, were not speaking. My aunt and uncle were debating where they went wrong—should they have sent Susan to a college in Michigan instead of that big university on the East Coast?

Guess Who's Coming to Dinner had recycled, that fall, through the campus cinema; already we hooted at its quaintness. I ordered another whiskey sour. I thought about villages burning in Cambodia and the sweet, nutty taste of Kevin Peters's hash pipe on the beach the week before and how exhilarating it was to finally, finally be living life as if it were a movie. My father spoke of "the possibility of children," as if mixed-race offspring were a genetic disease, like multiple sclerosis. He wanted to know if there was the remotest possibility that I would do something like what Susan had done. Because if so, he would have to. Well, he couldn't say. But he would come down hard. He would like to know. If there was a chance of this kind of accident.

"The black guys don't talk to me, Dad," I said. "I mean, it's not like *I* can ask *them* out, is it?"

I found this very funny. Not only because it used a dating expression—*ask them out*—but also at the idea of asking one of the black guys in my dorm to spend time with me. They had carefully groomed Afros. Their skin was all those colors I had read about, mahogany, coffee, molasses, Indian tea. They strutted around campus, their rib cages elevated, and looked at us white girls as though we were made of water. They did not hang out.

My choices for an escort, when you got down to it, were very few. I had lost my virginity the year before to a thoughtless senior. Since that time, hanging out had not produced the right chemistry—unless you counted Steve Erickson or Michael Edson, which I did not.

Nick Peterson, my philosophy professor, had at thirty-three published a groundbreaking work on Heidegger and been promoted to full professor. His marriage had broken up. He drove an orange BMW and flirted, like all the professors, with undergraduates. Not entirely immune to his charms, I was nonetheless incapable of imagining carnal relations between us. It astonished me that he would come knocking on my dorm room door on a Saturday morning to persuade me to lunch at the fancy Mexican restaurant up on Indian Hill Boulevard. It astonished me that he bought us margaritas and then sat there while I nibbled on a burrito. Too high-strung to eat, he instead slowly tore his napkin into shreds and recounted his sexual history to me. When the napkin was gone, he arranged the tortilla chips on his place mat—into stars, into pentangles, into origami ducks.

"You know," he said to me, sadly, "there are, in the end, only so many orifices one can enter."

I did not know what to say to this. After lunch, he dropped me back at my dorm and drove off. The girl next door and the tarantula girl gathered around, wanting to know what had happened.

"Nothing," I said. "He made shapes with his tortilla chips, just like last time."

My other visitor, Michael Edson, came from a prominent Jewish family in Chicago and had money to burn. I had met him only that year because he had spent my freshman year in Switzerland, studying transcendental meditation with Maharishi Mahesh Yogi. The year before that, while I was plotting my escape from St. Louis, he had roomed with the boy who was now in Europe and purportedly in love with me. All I knew of this other boy, actually, was that he had sat next to me in my class on the Bible as Literature. For his final paper, he had presented a play about Uzzah and the Lord. Uzzah was the Jew who had saved the Tabernacle of the Lord from falling to the ground during a parade in Jerusalem, and for his reward, he had been struck dead by God, who had decreed that none should touch his tabernacle. The boy had asked me to read it, and I thought it was a good play.

Now, during the fall of 1972, Michael Edson came around to discuss the play and the boy with me, and it seemed to me—though I was ignorant as a rock about matters of sexuality—that Michael was in love with this boy. From time to time, Michael professed desire for me, but this was a weak sentiment uttered as a conversation gambit, and we moved on easily to topics like the hallucinogenic qualities of tequila. Michael was tall and thin in a weak, hungry way, with a head that seemed larger than it really was because of long hair, a full beard, protuberant eyes behind thick glasses, and a Groucho nose. He sat on the floor of my dorm room smoking marijuana, and his head seemed too large and heavy for his neck to hold erect.

"Rod's in Vienna now," Michael said of the boy who was supposedly in love with me. "He's studying German opera. Can you imagine? I should have stayed over in Switzerland."

"Why didn't you?" I said.

"They were starving me! You're supposed to meditate seven hours a day. Then you're supposed to eat a black roll and a cup of tea. It's all very strict. Nobody has any sex. For six months I got no exercise at all, and my muscles totally atrophied. See?" he said, and showed me his thin legs. "It was an amazing experience. The Maharishi is a total fucking genius. I am a complete person like you'll never be. My mantra keeps me at peace. But they were going to kill me if I stayed."

Michael had passed enough stages at the school in Switzerland that he was now empowered to repair mantras, as he had done for a girl named Lynn, at our school. For weeks Lynn's mantra had been broken. She hadn't been able to eat or sleep. Her meditation went nowhere. Then Michael sat down with her and—he said—grokked, and fixed her mantra, and now she was back to her old cheerful self.

"You should learn to meditate," he told me. "If you won't have sex with me, at least you could meditate with me. You would be incredible."

"I don't want a mantra that gets broken," I said. "Right now I have no mantra, and I'm fine. A broken mantra sounds much worse than no mantra at all."

"I would fix it for you," said Michael.

"You would not be there," I said.

Michael smelled of marijuana, which he smoked continually, and of unwashed beard. I wished he would not come around, but it was he whom I ended up inviting to be my escort to the Veiled Prophet Ball.

Not inviting, exactly. Rather, in a gesture that heaped scorn at once upon the tradition of dating and the tradition of the ball, I announced at a party that I was seeking an escort and would promise a unique experience to anyone willing.

The party was at a professor's house, one of those occasions where students attempted to act wise and jaded and professors to act young and game. Nick Peterson was present, as was Michael. I was working hard not to care for anyone there. I had by now made my plans to escape again, this time across the waters, where neither my embarrassing society background nor my unsatisfactory liaisons, nor even my father's unsettling new marriage, nor anything that touched beneath my skin could reach me. And so I blithely told those assembled, on couches and ottomans and the blond carpeting of the professor's living room, about the ball.

"Every year," I said, stationing myself in the midst of the circle, "there occurs in my hometown a miracle."

Michael Edson, seated to my right and sipping tequila, snickered.

"His Mysterious Majesty," I said, "the Veiled Prophet, comes on his flying carpet from his magic land of Khorassan to his beloved city of St. Louis to crown his Queen of Love and Beauty. Whose father just happens to be the richest man in town that year."

Laughter all around. A joint passed; I took a toke. "Picture a large, public arena," I said. "Madison Square Garden. The Coliseum. Picture a private group closing it down for three weeks. They wrap the pillars in white bunting. They cover the seats with white padding. They lay down white carpet and a red runner going the length of the hall. They erect a fabulous stage, and a throne for the Prophet, and everywhere silken curtains and fabulous attendants. The trumpets sound. Then the Maids appear."

I stood. I was wearing a knit halter top and low-slung jeans; I was drunk and felt sexy. I had personality. Turning toward the professor's fireplace, I faked the blowing of a trumpet. "His Mysteeerious Majesty!" I said in my darkest, most rumbling voice, "the Vaaaayled Prrophet! Welcomes! To his Court! Of Love! And Beauty! Miss! Lucy! Ann! Ferriss!"

I turned. I took several steps backward, pushing aside the coffee table on which I'd been sitting, then I lifted my chin and stepped forward. "I've been practicing this," I explained to my ironic audience, "since seventh-grade dance class." I took another step and lifted my arms to the side. "Obeisance to the male prerogative," I said, and did the bow. All the way to the floor, right leg bent under left, neck curving swanlike forward. Then up again, no cracking of the knees, and my princess smile.

"Bravo!" said the professor hosting the party, a man in his forties who sported a goatee and an acquaintance with the works of Carlos Castaneda.

"That is so camp," said one of the students.

"I have to have an escort, though," I said. I looked around the room. "Anybody want to come to St. Louis?"

There was an awkward silence. I would have had more response asking them if they wanted to row to Catalina Island. Finally Michael spoke up. "It's on my way home to Chicago," he said.

And so Michael was the chosen one.

"What the hell is this Veiled Prophet, anyhow?" he asked the next time he brought a lid of marijuana over to my dorm room. "I mean, where did he come from, in the first place?"

I shrugged. "Beats me," I said.

Three

The Story

Mokanna.
That's his real name.
I have come to learn it in what seems a very different age, more than twenty-five years after the events of 1972. I live, now, on America's other coast. I teach literature. When in idle conversation I mentioned the Veiled Prophet to a colleague well versed in nineteenth-century Irish poetry, he did not say, "Oh yes, the St. Louis ball." He said, "Oh yes, *Lalla Rookh*."

Which, it turns out, is the title of an epic poem by the now-obscure Irish bard Thomas Moore, penned during the Orientalist fervor that swept through literature and the arts in the heyday of British imperialism. "Do you have it?" I asked my colleague. He rummaged on his shelf, found a volume, riffled through the pages, and handed me the chapter entitled "The Veiled Prophet of Khorassan." It begins thus:

> In that delightful Province of the Sun,
> The first of Persian lands he shines upon,
> Where all the loveliest children of his beam,
> Flow'rets and fruits, blush over every stream,
> And, fairest of all streams, the MURGA roves
> Among MEROU'S bright palaces and groves;
> There on that throne, to which the blind belief

Of millions rais'd him, sat the Prophet-Chief,
The Great MOKANNA.

"He was a real guy, you know," my learned friend said as I turned the page.

"Who?"

"The Veiled Prophet. Mokanna. Lived during the time of Mohammed, apparently. Somewhere in the opium regions. Are you all right?"

"I have to go check something," I said.

And so I have begun.

   ⌗ ⌗ ⌗

Among His Mysterious Majesty's many contributions to his Beloved City must be counted the gifts he bestowed on those whom he "commanded" to appear at his annual Court of Love and Beauty. These gifts have ranged from Lalique crystal vases to sterling-silver trays to gilt-edged walnut cigar boxes. The year I turned two, the secret organization that governed the ball had the inspiration to send, instead, a children's book.

The Coming of the Veiled Prophet was illustrated in pen and ink, just like my book of Bible stories, and seemed to serve the same purpose. Sitting by my bedside at night, my father read the tale to me in his reedy baritone. "Once upon a time," he read, "in the faraway land of Khorassan, there was a wise and kindly ruler known as the Veiled Prophet."

I didn't much like the story. It lacked plot. All the Veiled Prophet did, as far as I could see, was watch his "Krewe" dance, ride his carpet, and shower blessings, especially on St. Louis. At the end of the book he crowned his Queen, who looked vaguely like pictures of my Aunt Ann. I was more for Thumbelina and Stuart Little, small reckless creatures who had to face troubles in life. The Veiled Prophet took his place alongside the Old Testament Noah and the Do Bee of Romper Room, one of those dull people it would do you good to hear about.

But St. Louis parents like my father were glad for *The Coming of the Veiled Prophet*. For so long they had been retelling the story, trying to impress upon their children the specialness of St. Louis, the reasons why the parade and the ball and the man in the pointy hat were so important. Now here they had it in a slender blue volume, where the Prophet's chosen city was on a par with Bethlehem and the wisdom of his final choice, made in a high-ceilinged court wreathed with bunting, seemed even more self-evident than in that mess of a manger.

Something about the Thomas Moore poem has driven me back to my copy of the blue children's book, hidden in a box of dusty volumes, between *Little Women* and *Queer Stories for Boys and Girls.* When I set the two volumes side by side, it is like discovering a combination to an old, stubborn lock.

In Moore's version of the Veiled Prophet story, Mokanna is an evil white sorcerer who rapes innocent maidens. After enslaving his population, he commits a Jonestown-style mass poisoning, leaving the dark Arabian hero of the tale to kill his beloved accidentally when he finds her disguised in the Prophet's robes:

> Eager he darts to meet the demon foe,
> Who still across wide heaps of ruin slow
> And falteringly comes, till they are near;
> Then, with a bound, rushes on AZIM'S spear,
> And, casting off the Veil in falling, shows—
> Oh!—'t is his ZELICA'S life-blood that flows!

The poem's appeal lies in its Oriental racism and sexual masochism. Before she is killed, the raped heroine, Zelica, prays "that her transgression here / Was but a passage through earth's grosser fire / From which the spirit would at last aspire." Only in the corrupt lands of Araby, the genteel reader concludes, does such pure evil triumph.

Turning from Moore's bloody Orientalist fantasy to my night-time story book, I face two questions. First, will the Veiled Prophet of my childhood turn out to be the same fellow who rapes and pillages his way through Moore's poem? Second, does it matter?

The answer to the first question lies on the first page of the children's book. The drawings depict the sandman figure I remember so well. The authors' language, however, is pure Moore. The Irish poet, for instance, writes of the Prophet's "dazzling brow"; the 1956 book renders "the dazzling brilliance" of his "brow." In place of Moore's slave troops, who "for war's more terrible attacks, / Wield the huge mace and ponderous battle-axe," the 1956 authors have created a jolly scene, in which "White-robed troops, carrying bows and arrows, maces and battle-axes, formed a snowy background to the scene of gaiety."

Same snowy whiteness, same dazzling light, same battle-axes. Except that one set of maces makes for a kind of castanets accompanying the dance music, whereas the other carries the fullest weight of literary foreshadowing.

I have the books spread out on the floor. I sit back on my haunches. So the authors of the blue children's book had the violent epic before them and were consciously cribbing from it. They were not fooled, as I had been, into thinking that the original prototype of their Prophet was a slender Santa Claus or a beneficent Merlin.

I've turned the key in the lock, but I am still stumped. Literary sleuthing is what I do, as it were, for a living. Whether the resemblance between the two books matters is a more personal question. I need to consider not only what possible bearing the lineaments of the old poem had on the fanfare of 1956 but also the ways in which the Prophet had returned to demon status, according to people like Percy Green, by 1972. Even if the maces make music, Percy's people seemed to be saying, they are still maces.

❈   ❈   ❈

I dig a little deeper. *Lalla Rookh,* I quickly learn, was hardly obscure in its time. It was a best-seller, a fan-club book, a titillating household tale for lovers of the pleasurably horrid. By the year 1856, when Moore's works were collected, the epic poem was in its twentieth edition. It continued to sell briskly through the end of the century. Women particularly loved it. Americans adored it. They named their daughters Lalla; they attended parties clad in Orientalist robes. When a float featuring the Veiled Prophet of Khorassan appeared in the New Orleans Mardi Gras Parade of

1877, it provoked a frisson of familiarity among the crowds—sort of like featuring Darth Vader surrounded by attacking Jedi. A gentleman visiting from St. Louis, a former Confederate colonel by the swashbuckling name of Alonzo Slayback, could not help but take note—of the character, the crowds, the possibilities.

I make a note to follow Slayback, and return to the poem.

Its first lines draw us, like the female protagonist, into the deadly magnetic field of the Veiled Prophet:

> Between the porphyry pillars, that uphold
> The rich moresque-work of the roof of gold,
> Aloft the Haram's curtain'd galleries rise,
> Where through the silken net-work, glancing eyes,
> From time to time, like sudden gleams that flow
> Through autumn clouds, shine o'er the pomp below.—
> What impious tongue, ye blushing saints, would dare
> To hint that aught but Heav'n hath placed you there?

The Prophet's intrinsic splendor and mystery would at first seem to betoken either a secret kindness or, like Hawthorne's veiled pastor, a secret shame with which we'll identify in the end. Soon enough, however, we learn that, far from being more benign than he appears, Mokanna is nastier than the reader can possibly imagine. His "silver veil" symbolizes evil's tendency to hide behind dazzling trappings. In the tragic ending, bright evil triumphs over dark goodness, sexual manipulation over love, self-destruction over all. We are left with the chilling possibility that, in the ruined lands of the Caliph's dark people, the terror of whiteness may one day return.

Hardly wise and kindly. Yet, I find myself thinking, not an inappropriate fable for America's Veiled Prophet. Black is set against white. Power wins. The girl dies in the end, and the boy matures. The Prophet flies "at the head of myriads, blind and fierce / As hooded falcons, through the universe."

No wonder, I think, he came to visit us every year.

Four

Secession

*The original organizers were . . . public-spirited
St. Louisans who banded themselves together
in an unselfish spirit of anonymous benefaction
for the community as a whole.*

— ST. LOUIS GLOBE-DEMOCRAT, 1958

By 1972, flying into St. Louis's suburban airport had become
an exercise in reorientation. The new concourses were all
makeshift, the highways still under construction. The cranes
I saw from the plane were building new skyscrapers in Clayton,
and the great hole in the cluster of high-rise towers south of
downtown marked the spot where Pruitt-Igoe, the first federally
funded public housing project, used to stand before the St. Louis
Housing Authority began dynamiting the complex. Except for the
630-foot-high Gateway Arch at the waterfront, there remained few
landmarks by which to mark our descent.

Before the building of the Arch, St. Louis had styled itself as the
"city of three rivers"—the Missouri, the Mississippi, and the
Ohio—but in fact it lay primarily, in the shape of a boomerang,
below the Missouri and west of the Mississippi. White exodus was
pushing west into Chesterfield and north past the airport into the
towns of Hazelwood and Florissant, buffering the anomalous black
suburb of Kinloch.

The Arch itself was a new landmark, a shimmering hairpin by
the tresses of the Mississippi. Below it the waterfront was being,

according to Mayor Cervantes, "revitalized." Proud of his Spanish heritage, Mayor Cervantes had at one point convinced the city council to purchase not only the Spanish Pavilion from the New York World's Fair but also an eighty-foot-long replica of the *Santa Maria*, which was installed ceremoniously in the Mississippi River. The tourist draw had proved nil, the stock for ridicule limitless. It was a blessing when a tornado loosed the ship from its moorings one night and sent it down the Old Man to a watery grave. Still, the focus on the riverfront persisted, combined with the renewed notion of St. Louis as "Gateway to the West."

As I flew into St. Louis that December from my lotusland college life, I knew something of the sad history that attended my city, skewed though the lessons of that history had become. I knew, for instance, that no symbol could stop the bleeding of white money from the inner city. I knew that Lambert Field airport, outdated and overcrowded, was a bone of contention in the city's plea for life support from its surrounding county. Proposals, I had heard, were on the table to relocate the airport to a new structure across the river, in East St. Louis, a move that could not only resuscitate the Illinois side of the river but also force a link passing through the heart of downtown.

Everyone of my acquaintance was opposed to this idea. Let the city mind the city, they said; they were the ones who split off from us.

This was true. The city of St. Louis had indeed seceded from its county, long before there were airports or interstates. As a result, the city received no tax revenues from the burgeoning county, no support of its roads or municipal buildings, its parks or its schools.

"*Why* would the city want to split off from the county?" I used to ask my mother.

My mother shrugged. "They were stupid, I guess."

"They" were, to my mind, also black.

⌘ ⌘ ⌘

Nineteen seventy-two happened to be my year. Had it been otherwise, I might never find myself, now, flying back into Lambert Field, my address book filled with the coordinates of people I have never met. The fulcrum of my story is 1972, but the story itself spreads outward and backward from that year and that night and does not admit of strict chronology. I ought to be describing the parties that greeted my return home from college and the preparations for my father's wedding, two days before the ball. But there are other preparations and events that need, first, to be accounted for. There are other players: Percy Green and Margaret Phillips. The fairy godmothers, Jane Sauer and Gena Scott, who had not been invited to the ball. Laura Rand Orthwein, who had been invited but would not attend. There are other questions to be asked.

It is to ask these questions that I've returned in a bleak January, my curiosity pricked by *Lalla Rookh*. I am staying with neither of my divorced parents but instead in the "pool house" of a Mary Institute alumna. The house is hidden from the main road, on several well-tended acres. The elegant two-story bungalow where I'm ensconced sits between the pool and the tennis court, with the greenhouse beyond. The pool is kept running throughout the winter, the vacuum sweeping the water several times a day, both because it looks prettier that way and because pool covers are such a hassle. The main house is built hacienda-style, with one four-car garage on the side and another at the back of the property. My hosts are not home. They are taking a theater week at their apartment in New York City.

Money, of course, is not unique to St. Louis. By some standards, the estate where I've spread out my notes and books is not even an ostentatious home. The difference lies in my own recognition. I know this splendid place—or places just like it—from my childhood. These were the homes the other girls lived in, homes that were more than one house or so many cubic feet in an apartment building. These were multihouse homes that provided employment to a half-dozen people tending and pruning and cleaning and decorating and cooking.

There was a time when I thought I was supposed to have a home like this, up a winding drive with a sweep of lawn in front and marble statues in the living room. I thought a home like this would help me escape from what I perceived as the meanness of my life. Now, unpacking my small travel bag in the pool house of this midwestern palace has made me so nervous I cannot breathe right.

Not that I am poor, nor that I have ever known anything approaching poverty. For almost three decades now, I've been able to afford flying into St. Louis a couple of times a year. I have made my way here from airports on either end of the country, passing through cities known to me only by the quality of their interconcourse transportation systems. But this is the first time I have come to town and declined the guest beds at my mother's peach-colored apartment or my father's dark, heirloom-packed home. I am staying here rather than with one of my parents because I have come to St. Louis not to visit but to investigate. Just as I was afraid, twenty-seven years ago, to challenge my father by giving my tickets away to Percy Green, now I shun the prospect of staying in one or another household while I question the unquestionable. Instead I am raiding the stocked refrigerator of the pool house, taking strolls through the woods and onto the neatly groomed campus of John Burroughs School. I am squirreling myself away by the microfilm readers at the Missouri Historical Society, where I unravel some of the knots in my notion of history.

From old reports—in the narrow columns of Joseph Pulitzer's *St. Louis Post-Dispatch,* in the documents of the city government, and in the mammoth *History of St. Louis* penned in the 1930s—I learn that the secession of the city from the county took place in the 1870s, around the time of the founding of the Veiled Prophet Society. I learn that the secessionists and the veiled prophets were the same men. I learn that these city fathers feared the influx, not of another race, but of the poor farmers and idle speculators who scraped a living out of the lands rimming the then-wealthy city of St. Louis.

I go for walks in Forest Park. I make phone calls. I ask the librarian for more reels.

I learn of shortsightedness and of greed. I read the original charter, in which the founding fathers drew an imaginary line around what they saw as the utmost expanse of the city, out as far as the edge of the untamed acreage known as Forest Park. They decreed that every municipality outside that line would have to fend for itself, as the city would do.

I follow the course of history from that charter through the black northward migration of the 1920s. It was then, I realize, as the city of St. Louis unexpectedly filled with this new source of cheap labor, that the city fathers themselves jumped the line and began to settle in the unfettered county, abandoning the city they had once held so dear.

They were not black. They were white, and they had scampered away from the sinking ship.

⁜   ⁜   ⁜

In 1972, as I flew into Lambert Field, these runes of history lay beyond my ken. I knew only that, in my short lifetime, the city of St. Louis had lost almost a quarter of a million inhabitants. I knew only that the city's share of the greater metropolitan population had fallen from more than half to scarcely a fourth. I did not know that St. Louis boasted the nation's highest infant mortality rate or one of its highest rates of black joblessness. I knew only that skyscrapers were being razed downtown and rising like Phoenixes from the plains out toward the belt highway.

It was happening everywhere, I told myself as we landed at Lambert Field. But it seemed to me it was happening faster in St. Louis, and I felt ashamed, as if the rest of the world were managing to tread water while we, poor swimmers, sank from view.

⁜   ⁜   ⁜

There were other types of secession. My father's second marriage, for instance, which I had arrived in time to celebrate. I was staying at my mother's new house, out on Maryhill Lane in Ladue. My father was a canary, my mother a hornet. "You haven't said a thing about this house!" she cried, the day after I arrived.

I glanced around. "It looks nice," I said.

This was not the right thing to say. It betrayed the sad fact that I had been oblivious to the new house; oblivious, when it came to that, to the selling of the old house, the disposal of furnishings, and the painful relocation away from Clayton and into a subdivision in Ladue, just up the hill from Mary Institute, the school my sister still attended.

I had loved our old house. A rambling, white frame with a sloping front lawn suitable for sledding, it sat comfortably on the edge of Clayton toward University City. But my mother had sold it after the divorce in favor of a brick ranch of which the realtor must have said, "Location, location, location." I had lived in this ranch house the previous summer, and in the intervening months my mother had effected miracles—transforming a mudroom into a sunny back den, refinishing the floors, replacing tacky light fixtures with small, graceful chandeliers and sconces. But my own life absorbed all my attention, and at its perimeters lay grief and rage at the dynamiting of our family.

So no, I had not said a thing about the house.

"Go ahead," my mother said, softening. "Show off your dress. Let's see what you got in California."

Despite having bought it under the influence of sherry and my hippie friends, I truly loved my dress. I knew it broke one of the clothing rules that my mother had set for me, but I thought its merits overcame that shortcoming.

The rule it broke was purple. I ought not to wear purple, my mother had cautioned me in high school, because it made my skin look sallow. Likewise, I was not to wear low scoop necks that exposed my unsightly collarbone. V-necks drew attention to my weak chin. Dirndl skirts poofed out in front and made me look as if I had a belly. My hair must be kept trimmed above the shoulders lest anyone see how thin and fine it was. Best not to pull it back, either, for fear I might expose my ears, which stuck out a bit, though not as badly as Dan's, which had been pinned back when he was young. I looked fairly attractive in shirtwaists. I did a funny thing with my mouth that made me look unattractive. I must never wear high heels, which made me taller than any boy I would ever have the luck to meet.

I thought the dress made the grade, except for the purple top— and it was a *light* purple, I was prepared to argue, a lavender really. But as I emerged from my new, narrow bedroom in the ranch house on Maryhill to model my ball gown, my mother's face fell.

"It has long sleeves," she said. Then she said, "The top is *knit*."

"Don't you think it's pretty?" I said.

"You can't wear long white gloves with that, Lucy," she sighed.

She put away a rectangular box that she had pulled out while I was changing and rummaged about in the front hall cupboard. "You can try these," she said, pulling out a smaller box.

Long white gloves! Suddenly I was seized with the desire to sheath my arms in the coolness of white cotton, the buttons that fastened around the elbow. What had I deprived myself of? "I'm sorry," I said, as I fitted the short pair on. "I didn't think about gloves."

"And we'll have to get you a padded bra. Don't argue with me," she said, holding up a hand. The iron in her voice masked her deep disappointment. More than a hundred dollars! And her daughter had come up with a clown gown!

"Whatever you say, Mom." Oh, I was a terrible daughter. I had proffered not a single compliment for her renovated den, her fixtures, or the freshly painted kitchen; I had never learned to date, and I would be forever a source of anguish and despair. "But look," I tried, more to keep the tears from spilling out of her eyes than to salvage my pride, "how the skirt moves when I turn. It's really special, Mom. Look."

That afternoon, I bought the bra at Famous-Barr. It made my breasts look like apples. I glanced longingly at the formal-wear department but did not venture close. Once you have seceded, there is no peaceful way back.

Five

The Wedding

Youth, both Black and White, throughout the entire United States have been revolting against their parents as such. What about you?

— LETTER FROM PERCY GREEN, CHAIRMAN OF
THE CIVIL RIGHTS GROUP ACTION, 1969

Everything about my family, it seemed to me at my father's wedding, was ridiculous. Our quarrels, our ceremonies, our arrangements. Here stood my dignified, foolish father, marrying Nancy Lacey, a thirty-six-year-old mother of two and the ex-wife of my philandering high school history teacher. We had cornered the Midwest market on farce.

My father's decision to remarry was not the issue. For twenty years my parents had coexisted like a Siamese cat and an English hunting dog, natural enemies. Sensing an opportunity, I had tried to style myself as the kind of woman my father might love—a sort of Wordsworthian companion, musical and meditative. When this approach met with indifference from my father, I leaped the divide and hissed at him from my mother's flank.

Take, for instance, the trip to Europe. Five years earlier, my mother had emptied the bank account into which she had deposited all her wages from working at McDonnell Douglas and had taken our family on a three-week tour. We spent five days at Schliersee, an Alpine lake, and my father and I hiked the small mountain on the other side. Stopping at a hut, we drank citron together. We talked about how thirsty we were and how beautiful the mountain was. At the top, we sat side by side, silently communing. No one else in our family had cared to discover this splendor, just we two.

That night I ordered venison for the first time but couldn't eat the rich meat. My father launched a tirade about wasting expensive food. My sister set down her fork and stared at her lap. My mother lit a cigarette. My father leaned across the table, shaking a finger at me, and the day on the mountain dissolved into dust.

I drew myself up. "You have nothing to say about the money I spend," I said. "Mother paid for this trip, not you."

"That's not true," he rejoined hotly. "I contributed my share."

"A thousand dollars," I sneered. "That barely buys us breakfast."

He glanced from me to my mother, threw down his napkin, and left the table.

Every family has its own set of myths. In my family's central myth, my mother had married up and was concerned with the practical side of life. My father had married for love and revered life's finer points—history, music, beauty. My mother was an atheist, my father Episcopalian; my mother a lover of parties, my father of nature. And because my father was discriminating, whereas my mother was undiscriminating, the affection for which I played was my father's.

To gain it, I had sung in the children's choir, taken piano lessons, memorized poetry, and learned French, which he had loved speaking during the Second World War. When I fainted from the heavy robes and hot lights in the choir stalls, he supplied me with smelling salts. When I faltered at piano, he took to accompanying me to my lessons, where he sat, grim and silent, in the corner. Mostly, I did not measure up, but I persevered. In my fondest recollections of my father, we are canoeing down a stream in the Ozarks, and, for a few hours, we are soul mates of nature (Wordsworth!) and of one another. These moments are framed by a vexed narrative in which I line up one accomplishment after another in hopes of my father's approval.

My father, as it turned out, did not yearn for a daughter of accomplishment or taste or any of the values he held dear. We were, after all, faded aristocracy. As a circuit judge, my father would never own the sort of home in which he had grown up. Hadn't he given up the country club to afford having me? As much as anything else, the status of his two sisters—both well-married, affluent women of accomplishment—reproved him for his own failure to maintain his status. As I moved through puberty, I noticed how often he called me by his sisters' names, and how I resembled them physically. He teased me for fiddling with my hopeless hair; he teased me about my small breasts. I sat to his right at the dining table, and if my elbow strayed onto its surface, he flicked it off as if it were a gnat. I ate slowly, and he was always hungry. "Looks like more than you can handle," he would say, as he reached across to fork the last of my ham.

I understood that my father resented me for the very qualities that I had labored to acquire. And I was furious. It was that fury that provoked the retort, so like my mother's: "A thousand dollars! That barely buys us breakfast." I wanted him to know that I was unimpressed by his pedigree and untouched by his mockery and small criticisms; that I cared nothing for his praise.

By flying out to college in California, I proved I was nothing like his sisters and nothing like the daughter he ought to have had, the one that went to Wellesley or to Sweet Briar. During the hot summer of 1972, I trudged door-to-door in snooty Ladue, selling Avon cosmetics, rather than accept the camp-counseling job that Franklin Ferriss's influence had helped me nail the two previous summers.

At the same time, when my father had advised me that Radcliffe was where the brainy girls went—*brainy* a term laced with poison— I had put that application aside. Still and always, I wanted to be the daughter he loved.

A counselor my father and I had seen several times when I was in my early teens had ended by asking me how many more years I would be living at home. When I said four, he said, "Then in four years you'll be free of him. That's the best advice I can give."

⌗   ⌗   ⌗

Now that he was remarrying, I supposed, I was free. It had been almost two years since he had lost his volatile temper at my mother over a department-store charge, and my mother, who was fixing supper, had brandished a chopping knife at him. He had fled the house. Six months later, they were mercifully divorced.

Which was fine, my brother and I said, with us. We liked the idea of our curmudgeonly dad as an eligible bachelor. For a time, very shortly after the split, he had dated Betty Masters, ex-wife of William Masters, part of the renowned team of sex therapists known as Masters and Johnson. Betty Masters would do fine, we said. Let him remarry; and soon.

But Nancy Lacey was not what we had in mind. Her husband had lost his post at Mary Institute because he had carried on a clandestine affair with a scholarship girl in my class. We all thought Brad Lacey was slimy, and, by implication, anyone who had borne his children had to be slimy too.

To make matters worse, Nancy was religious in the same way my father was religious. They were both devout, church-going Episcopalians who had met through Sunday school training. That year, they were both earnest in their defense of Missouri's blue laws, and my father's Chevrolet sported a bumper sticker reading "Save Our Sundays!"

Although my reply to Percy Green's letter had cited the debt that I owed my father, I did not stop to wonder how the entrance of this pious, wronged schoolteacher in my father's life changed the terms of that debt. No longer could I angle for my father's affections by being different from his patrician sisters or his tart ex-wife. And who said I was angling for his affections anyway? I was free of him. Yet here was Nancy Lacey and, in my heart, a sinking sense of loss.

※　※　※

The ceremony was held in the small chapel of the enormous church where I had been reluctantly confirmed in the faith, at the inner edge of St. Louis County near Forest Park. It was the church my father had attended as a child, one of those dark high-ceilinged sanctuaries that resemble an upturned ark. Officiating was John C. Danforth, then a young minister. Tall, hawk-nosed, and handsome, with a shock of white caused by a patchy loss of pigment in his otherwise sable hair, he seemed to me a kind of St. Louis Kennedy.

I couldn't imagine that such a charismatic young man would enter the ministry. The Episcopal ministry, no less. "Jack's got political ambitions," my father had said with a wink. (Truly spoken: Senator Danforth's fame would come a couple of decades later, with his successful championing of Clarence Thomas for the U.S. Supreme Court. His hair, by then, matched his early pigmentation.)

The ceremony lasted a long while. Nancy wore a blue suit. She was a pale, attractive woman with an athletic laugh and an unsettling stare from behind her glasses. My father spoke his lines with a practiced conviction. Not far from me in the pews, my step-grandmother, Grace Davies Ferriss, sat stiff and elegant in a netted hat on her head and a designer scarf around her neck. She was the only grandmother I had known, but she had married my widowed grandfather two years after my birth, and she did not, in most ways, conform to the image others had of my father's family. She had led a sophisticated international life; she had once dated Douglas Fairbanks Sr; her views were those of New York and London. It was well known that she disapproved of my father's nuptials on the unapologetic grounds of social class. Reportedly, she had sat him down a few months earlier, when he and Nancy Lacey had announced their plans to wed. "Love her," she had said to him. "Sleep with her. Live with her if you must! But Franklin, do not *marry* her."

My father had thanked her for the advice and gone ahead with his plans. Many years before—or so I had heard—he had had a girlfriend named Mary, who had a glass eye. On that basis, or so it seemed (she was always known as "Mary with the glass eye"), Mary did not garner the approval of my grandfather, and my father ceased courting her. Marrying Nancy Lacey, one could argue, was the single greatest act of rebellion in his long life. No wonder he stood proud and erect at the altar rail.

Afterward, there was a buffet lunch at Nancy's house on Arundel Place, where her two impossibly young sons ran between everyone's legs. My father accepted congratulations and reminded everyone who stepped forward that he was doubly blessed this Christmas season. Not only had he taken his Nancy to wed, but his daughter was to be presented in just three days at his Mysterious

Majesty's ball. These well-wishers turned from my father to me. I smiled, feeling fraudulent. The one I knew best was Hugh Scott, a genial businessman who resembled Henry Fonda. I asked after his daughter, Phoebe.

"Wishes she were here," he said.

"Really," I said, glancing at my father and Nancy.

"Don't worry! You'll do fine." He put his hand on my shoulder. "Phoebe was nervous as a cat," he said.

※　　※　　※

I imagined she was—but then Phoebe, two years earlier, had been the Queen. Before that, for six years at Mary Institute, we had shared a car pool. Our mothers drove their boatlike Ramblers and Plymouths through the curving, densely wooded streets of University City (named for Washington University), then out Pershing Boulevard, where the streetcars used to run, and finally up narrow, elegantly congested Ladue Road where medallions for private subdivisions—Ladue Acres, Sunnymeade, and Graybridge—dotted the unexpected intersections. I shrank into the backseat while Phoebe and her best friend, plump blond Meg Jolley, sang camp songs and made fun of their boyfriends.

Phoebe's crowning as Queen of Love and Beauty in 1970 had attested to her father's success in the business world. More to the point, she had agreed to a preball dialogue, in the kitchen of the Scotts' home, with my newfound correspondent, Percy Green. And the one who had arranged the dialogue had been none other than my Marxist Latin teacher, Margaret Phillips.

※　　※　　※

My 1969 Mary Institute yearbook shows Margaret Phillips by the fireplace in the Alumnae Room. She wears a short-sleeved, square-shouldered shirtwaist in a pattern of miniature flowers. Flanking her are Miss Adams, Mrs. Gieselmann, and Mrs. Pearson, whose ages average to perhaps sixty-two. The three older women are not smiling, though Mrs. Gieselmann has arranged her mouth to look kindly. They wear cardigan sweaters and dark skirts, and they have no noticeable waists. Their hair is softly waved and sprayed in place.

Miss Phillips's hair is cropped short like a boy's, the bangs a straight fringe across her forehead. The tentative curl to her lips makes her look as though she is following instructions that the others can't hear. She has stepped, you might say, into the wrong picture.

Margaret Phillips left after that year. They said she had been fired, like our math teacher Beau Birdwell, for doing unseemly things.

⌘ ⌘ ⌘

A quarter century after my father's wedding, I find myself sitting in Professor Margaret Phillips's small office at the University of Missouri, in the north end of St. Louis County. Her window gives onto the carefully seeded, amoeba-shaped patches of lawn peculiar to late-twentieth-century universities, with a huge parking complex off to one side and frail trees, supported by wires and rubber hoses, waving like thin children along the edges of curving walks. Professor Phillips now teaches both classical languages and criminology; the latter specialty is an interest born of her attempts to defend herself in 1970s civil disobedience cases. Her hair's grown, she tells me, to her waist, though she keeps it tied up in a steel-gray braid wrapped around her head—reminiscent no longer of the androgynous sixties radical but more of a nineteenth-century schoolmarm. The wide vowels of the South still come out in her speech, sharpened at the edges with midwestern consonants. She scarcely remembers me, though she has vivid recollections of Phoebe Scott and—to my surprise—of my father. I am also surprised, as former students often are, to discover how close we are in age and curious to trace the path she followed to the events of 1972.

"*My* father," she tells me, "was known as Red Ned the Wild Celt."

This was at the Citadel, that bastion of military education in Charleston, South Carolina. Although he was teaching future Army officers, Ned Phillips considered himself a political liberal. In the evening, his friends would come over, and they would argue about civil rights or the college's repressive administration. But Professor Phillips was a genteel sort of liberal, one that stayed within the system and discussed issues rationally. Margaret's home in South Carolina was a safe haven for free thought, connected by that thought to a world that was cataclysmically changing.

In 1965, the year Percy Green began organizing protests against the Veiled Prophet Ball, Margaret left first for Greece, then to enroll at the University of Chicago in classical languages.

"Chicago radicalized me," she says with assurance.

"But you took that job at Mary Institute," I say. "A private school; an elite place."

She raises her eyebrows.

"Conservative," I say.

"I was young," she says. "It was my first real job. I didn't have a clue what I was doing. The school reminded me of the place I'd attended as a girl. I thought I'd feel comfortable, teaching there. I thought I could separate my academics from my politics."

We reminisce about the school, the elderly teachers, the British headmaster, and about my favorite math teacher, Beau Birdwell.

"Such a sweet, gentle man," Margaret says.

I remember Mr. Birdwell as bald, plump, and ingratiating. Now I learn that he was weighed down by his marriage to a manic-depressive but in love with numbers and with music. Margaret's first year at Mary Institute, Beau was picked up one evening by under-cover police. They had spotted a known drug dealer coming to sit next to him at a table in a jazz bar in Gaslight Square, a downtown area famous for starting the careers of blues greats Chuck Berry and B. B. King. By the time the police had questioned Beau and let him go, the press had got hold of the story. The next morning, the school fired him. I remember my parents saying, "Where there's smoke there's fire."

"We tried to protest," says Margaret. "Some of the faculty voiced objections. But nothing changed." She rests her chin in her hand and looks out at the sterile view. "Beau's marriage broke up over it," she says.

I don't tell Margaret Phillips what a terrible Latin teacher I'd thought she was. By tenth grade I'd been ready to quit Latin. I had no aptitude for it and little interest. Per my mother's instructions, I was avoiding all markers of potential braininess. But the school's college adviser, ever fretting about the percentage of Mary Institute graduates who made it into Seven Sisters schools, insisted I sign on for Cicero. Dread changed to relief only when I discovered, along with the five other remaining Latin students in the tenth grade, that the new teacher could be sidetracked. We took pixie-haired Miss Phillips outside. We sat her down on the broad steps of the school entrance with its Ionic pillars or on the wrought-iron benches of the Alumnae Garden. We learned quickly that we could drop Cicero and take up Marx. All semester we talked about the theory of class. We praised the late Dr. Martin Luther King, whom our parents had not abided. I loved it. When I walked into the final exam and actually saw a passage of Cicero, I burst into tears. Later, when we all pulled Bs, we concluded that Miss Phillips had abandoned, along with other bourgeois hierarchies, the idea of grades.

"I always thought," I tell her, these many years later, "you'd been fired."

"If it had been drugs or sex, they'd have gotten rid of me without a second thought," says Margaret calmly. "Look at poor Beau. But they didn't pay too much attention to political action. They thought I was so green, nothing I could do would matter. No, I left on my own."

She had met George Johnson, a civil rights worker who lived in her apartment building. Margaret and George talked about religion and about the church in South Carolina where Margaret had gone as a child. George took her to St. Stephens Episcopal Church, down by Pruitt-Igoe, where half the large congregation belonged to a group called ACTION, founded by a young black activist named Percy Green.

Margaret's involvement with ACTION lasted only about three years. Still, her name pops up everywhere in the literature. In 1971, she and a fellow protester named Gena Scott breached security at McDonnell Douglas Corporation, where my mother worked. The two women's purpose was to draw attention, in true ACTION style, to job discrimination based on race. Although they were certainly aware that McDonnell was involved in military projects, theirs was not a war protest. Rather, they thought media coverage of a break-in would be bigger than coverage of a demonstration outside the complex, and so the issue of discrimination would come to the fore. Almost by accident, they penetrated as far as the room where the plans were kept for the F-15 fighter bomber. After being arrested, Margaret and Gena ended up in a criminal court-room presided over by Judge Franklin Ferriss.

Margaret looks abashed, telling me this story. "I wanted to do whatever I could to stop something that I saw as big and bad," she says. "It wasn't about Vietnam. It was about jobs."

Gena Scott asked for another venue because a McDonnell Douglas calendar hung in my father's chambers. My father said, as if it would remove any thought of influence, "Well, my wife just works at McDonnell." And so the trial went on, with the two women gamely defending themselves. Margaret remembers my father as surprisingly kind, casting significant looks at her when it was a good moment to raise an objection. Putting one another on the stand, the two women got a hung jury.

"My father doesn't remember the trial," I tell Margaret.

She shrugs. "It was a long time ago."

"I remember it, though. I remember you went from my dad's courtroom to Judge Rickhoff's."

"Rickhoff, yes," says Margaret. "He threw the book at us."

But she doesn't say the name the way my father did. My father used to roll the R of *Rickhoff* and cough the k. At the second syllable, he gave a quick derisive shake of his head. There was a great rivalry among the judges. My father liked to say he, too, had thrown the book at people.

After I meet with Margaret, I go back to the *Post-Dispatch* clipping. "It is a shame," my father is quoted as saying, "because now there will have to be a new trial with all that expense." Being judicial, he says nothing about the ethics of a break-in at McDonnell Douglas. In my memory he never has a kind word to spare for McDonnell Douglas. He did not want his wife to work there, or anywhere.

❊ ❊ ❊

As I shook Hugh Scott's hand at my father's wedding, I thought of Miss Phillips—of her failed Latin classes, of the trial in my father's courtroom, but mostly of the kitchen meeting between Percy Green and Phoebe Scott. I knew Miss Phillips had arranged the confrontation because news of it had run in the *Post-Dispatch* the day after the 1970 Veiled Prophet Ball. The interview itself had taken place three weeks before the ball, when neither Margaret Phillips nor anyone outside the inner circle knew that Phoebe was slated to be Queen. Miss Phillips had chosen her only because she was willing, and because she had been an excellent student in Latin.

The photo in the newspaper had flattered Phoebe; Percy was no more than a dark oval under the mushroom of his beret. To the *Post-Dispatch* reporter Phoebe had said, "He expressed his point of view, we ours. I don't think any of us changed our minds." Hugh Scott had stayed in the kitchen throughout the interview, his eyes riveted on his daughter.

Now he moved among my father's guests, this man whose wealth or power, or fund of favors owed, had earned his daughter a tiara, as my grandfather had done for—or to—my Aunt Ann. I disapproved of the whole business and was bursting with jealousy.

I watched Hugh Scott work the room, extending his hand, touching women on their elbows and slapping men on their shoulder blades. People like Hugh Scott and Margaret Phillips, it seemed to me, knew who they were. Wherever they stood, they knew how they were expected to act, what the stakes were. My family—my father—had never really learned the game.

Champagne was being poured. Light reflected off Nancy Lacey's— now Nancy Ferriss's—glasses. Outside it was raining, a damp St. Louis Christmas season. I wondered where Michael Edson was. I hoped no one would crack McGovern jokes. I prayed I would look pretty in my dress.

Six

The Invitations

Wherever the appearance of a conventional
aristocracy exists in America, it must arise
from wealth, as it cannot from birth.

— HARRIET MARTINEAU, *Society in America*, 1837

O n my fourth day in the pool house, I drive my rental car
downtown, to the St. Louis Mercantile Library. The
collections of the Mercantile, I have been told, house all
the clippings relevant to each visit by the Veiled Prophet to his
Beloved City, as well as all the documents critical to the "city
fathers" of the 1870s. The Mercantile is also a study in the devolu-
tion of St. Louis. When I arrive to do research, dozens of boxes are
piled by the closely guarded entrance. The library is packing up to
move to a University of Missouri campus in the county.

For the moment, though, the banker's lamps and polished desks
are still in place. In the library's hushed reading room, I dig up the
clippings about my aunt Ann and the Queens who came before her.
On the warm oak table, I spread the news from 1877, 1904, 1956,
and 1972. The librarian handling my requests notices the coinci-
dence of names and says, "Why, are you Ann Ferriss's daughter?"

"Her niece," I say.

"Such a lovely tradition," says the librarian. She shakes her head
fondly. "The girls are always so well brought up. It's like a fairy tale,
really."

"You could say that," I say.

Ann Chittenden Ferriss. Veiled Prophet Queen, 1931. Photo taken in the library of her family home. (Photo courtesy of the Missouri Historical Society)

"Such a shame," says the librarian. Her eyes stray around the amber-lit, high-ceilinged room as if we were suddenly discussing the library's imminent relocation. "Such a shame that people can't leave things alone."

From the Mercantile Library I take photocopies of memorabilia from 1931, the year my young, blond, slender aunt was crowned Queen—photos of the ball itself, a copy of the invitation, a biography of my grandfather, and a posed portrait of Ann in her father's study. She stands before an oval mirror and a wall of bookshelves topped by candelabra. Her hair is cropped and crimped close to her head, in the style of the time. She holds a gargantuan bouquet of autumn flowers. The train of her gown—"ruby and gold lamé, designed on princess lines, flaring from the knee . . . the main part heavily embroidered in gold, the bodice, which has a broad round neckline in front and a deep V in the back, being done entirely of ruby and gold jewels. From the waistline in the back extend two graceful narrow trains of gold lace, falling over a lamé train. Over the whole hangs a regal train of ruby velvet, magnificently embroidered in gold and lined with gold lamé"—the train flows in front and around her like an enormous, multitextured lily pad.

The materials from the library are endless. There are financial records from the St. Louis Agricultural and Mechanical Fair, from which the Veiled Prophet sprang. There are portraits of former Queens, including the one who had married in secret and was therefore run out of town, and the one who, soon after marrying an Italian count, slit her wrists. There is the photo of my aunt on my ecstatic father's arm, parading as one of the former Queens in 1981. I lose track of what I am seeking. Leaving my materials in the good hands of the librarian, I take a walk for lunch.

There is nowhere to eat in this part of downtown. I don't mean nowhere decent to eat—I mean nowhere. I walk a labyrinth of perhaps ten blocks in the damp chill. The buildings are all square, dozen-storied, brick or stone artifacts, with gargoyles occasionally leering from crumbling cornices. Corner grocery stores are boarded up; signs in front of defunct diners hang off rusting braces. Building directories list bail bondsmen, tattoo artists, and printers. I feed the meter by my car; then I notice that the meters by the other cars are all expired. A dozen storefronts are boarded up and graffitied. Through the space between buildings I glimpse the north foot of the Arch. I consider driving somewhere to eat. Tonight I will be having supper at my mother's apartment, and it is never a good idea to arrive hungry at my mother's. But when I circle around by the main entrance of the library again, I give up and reenter. Perhaps, I think, the library employees all bring sandwiches. Perhaps they huddle in a little room somewhere, with vending machines. I leaf through my research materials, but I cannot escape this new vision of my home city as a collection of half-empty offices with dirty windows in which the stubborn remaining few wash down braunschweiger sandwiches with a warm Bud.

On my way to my mother's, I pick up a slice of St. Louis's specialty, Gooey Butter Coffee Cake, and devour it. The reason not to arrive hungry is that my mother serves delicate portions of food, and, when one requests seconds, she exclaims, "Why, you're eating enough for an *army*." Even now, I cannot abide the accusation of consuming like the military. The Gooey Butter anchors my stomach and makes everything else unnecessary. That evening I eat like a princess, leaving food on my plate. After supper my mother fetches a box from her study.

"If you're going to be writing about it," she says, setting the box down on her glass coffee table, "you may as well have these. My mother saved them. I've saved them. Now it's up to you."

☷   ☷   ☷

So here is my first real discovery. I unwrap the package at my mother's apartment, only to wrap it back up and then open it again at the pool house. What she has saved for me are a couple dozen Veiled Prophet Ball invitations, stretching back over the last century, and they take my breath away. It is impossible not to admire them.

The oldest invitation is from 1885, the eighth year of the ball. Its "envelope" is an ivory silk pouch, six inches wide, pointed like a bishop's miter on the bottom and lined in burgundy silk, with five matching burgundy tassels; two of the tassels pull on a cord to cinch the top. Bisecting a printed green maple branch on the front of the pouch is an oval image of the Prophet. From the back of his

Invitation to the Veiled Prophet Ball, 1885.

lowered head, his translucent veil sweeps over his face until it blends with his long white beard. He looks burdened, pensive, like Moses; the maple branch could be his burning bush.

Out of the silk pouch I pull an intricately folded square of thick stationery, which also has the image of the Prophet and the maple branch printed on it. Untying the silk ribbon that seals the paper, I extract the invitation, a folded, gilt-edged card. Glued to the front is a square duotone lithograph that is hidden behind three hinged ovals that overlay the image from the corners. All three of the ovals depict the same Arabian-looking figure, with pointy shoes and curved sword, but they are of different scenes—the first shows the figure receiving a gleaming art-deco vision of armor; the second is of him being hoisted aloft on his carpet by a fantastic bird of prey; and in the third, mermaids accompany him to a tropical island. The last oval lifts to reveal a seated young woman, presumably Scheherazade of *A Thousand and One Nights,* faced by her pudgy turbaned bodyguard, his scimitar at the ready. According to a small caption on the inside of the invitation, these illustrations are from "Arabian Nights." Also inside is the troubled Prophet and these elaborately bedizened words:

> *The pleasure of your company*
> *is requested at the*
> *Eighth Annual Festival*
> *of the*
> *Veiled Prophets*
> *October 6th 1885*
> *at Chamber of Commerce*
> *St. Louis*

Enclosed in the invitation are two identical cards, equally elaborate, with "Mr. and Mrs. A. W. Smith" (my mother's maternal grandparents) written in a distinguished script and the notes "Personal and Not Transferable" and "Costume de Rigueur."

The following year's invitation I leave out overnight, anticipating its greeting me in the morning. Although the custom-made

Invitation to the Veiled Prophet Ball, 1885.

Top, invitation to the Veiled Prophet Ball, 1885.
Bottom, invitation to the Veiled Prophet Ball, 1886.

triangular envelope bears a two-cent stamp, my mother swore the invitation arrived by hand. In addition to the beautifully penned address (the third line reads simply "City"), the envelope bears the number "213," presumably its place in the pecking order. From the open bottom of the envelope I slip out what appears to be a triangular book, wrapped in brown paper, with Arabic-looking characters scrolled on the flap and an Arabic-looking red seal closing the wrap.

As if I were opening Chinese boxes, I come upon another book-ish triangle, this time in maroon leatherette, the flap folded and tucked into a small crease toward the point of the triangle. I open the flap again, and this time the invitation proper slides out. Here, the triangle opens first into a larger triangle of silk-covered card paper, engraved in gilt with the words "St. Louis Chamber of Commerce, Oct. 5, 1886, Veiled Prophets," and a few more Arabic characters. On the left half of the triangle is the gilt Prophet, again in an oval, somber but less downhearted this time, staring soberly ahead, with his chain-mailed arms holding aloft a half-unrolled scroll that one might take for the Code of Hammurabi. On the right, pairing the Prophet, is William Shakespeare, equally somber, staring, and pointing toward an enormous globe, to a spot that seems to be somewhere in the middle of America. Both figures are backlit by centripetal lines, like a burst of light behind each man's head.

The triangles open further, inviting me to turn over to what is now a diamond of four triangular, full-color images, reading clockwise. The first, top right, captioned "Palos 1492," shows Christopher Columbus standing on a stone quay in Spain pointing out to an astounded *conquistador* the three ships that lie waiting for him far off in the harbor. Top right, "San Salvadore 1492" shows the same ships, now offshore of a tropical island, with three colorful Indians in the foreground gazing back at them. One savage, standing with spear and leather shield, looks ready to take on the intruders; another sits on a rock in Rodin's thinker's pose, already resigned; the third, a woman with a child to her naked breast, is about to flee in terror. Pivoting the card, I find "The Mississippi 1541," where the savages' attitude has changed: they now offer a peace pipe and baskets of produce to the splendid Spanish officers

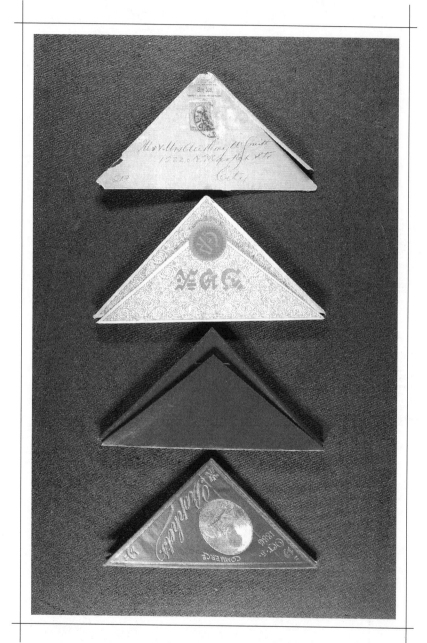

Invitation to the Veiled Prophet Ball, 1886.

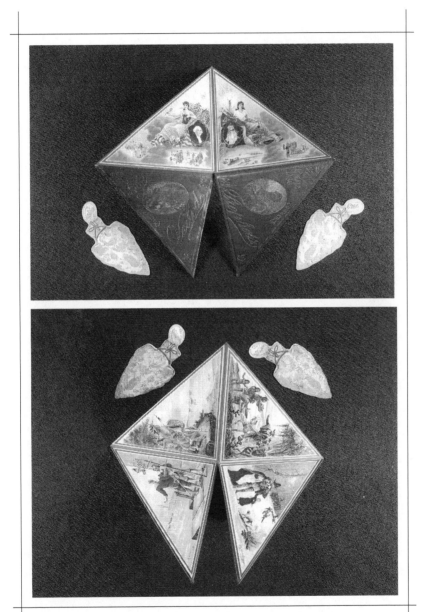

Invitation to the Veiled Prophet Ball, 1886.

and the missionaries close behind, with Spanish moss dropping from the canopy of trees overhead. Finally, "Plymouth 1620" shows a Pilgrim family (the black-hatted father, musket on his shoulder, bears a keen resemblance to Shakespeare on the reverse) huddled about a blazing fire in the snow while industrious comrades build a log house in the background.

Flipping the card back, I find a pair of images to sum up the story. In the right triangle sits a Grecian-style lady on a robe of the American flag, her left elbow lightly resting on a framed portrait of George Washington. In one hand she holds a book, in the other a pen. Above her head—backlit, like the first image, by the rising sun—floats the date 1776. In the coffee-colored clouds below her are two miniature tableaux—of Washington addressing Congress and of winter on the Potomac. At her feet lie a pair of American Beauty roses. Her partner, in the right-hand triangle, is more modern-looking—her face slightly sharper, her hair curled around her shoulders. The robe on which she reclines boasts the red and gold of the Prophet; the Grand Oracle himself stares wistfully from the frame on which she leans. In her right hand is the eagle scepter, in her left a goblet that (in contrast to the sun) supplies the light above her head. The date above her head is 1886, and, instead of roses, two spools of electrical wire lie at her feet. The tableaux in the clouds represent the railroads and the telephone, proclaiming the material progress of a century.

The admission cards are in the form of arrowheads, the size and shape of the ones we used to hunt on trips to the Ozark Mountains. The one for the gentleman is painted with a blue ribbon; the one for the lady, with a red. Weapons transformed, by Will and George and the Grand Oracle, into tokens for the ball.

They go on and on—invitations in the form of Chinese folding puzzles; invitations like full-color lithographs to frame and hang on your wall; invitations featuring the Prophet rising like Neptune from the azure depths of an endless sea; and invitations with a younger, more Clark Gable–like Prophet hypnotizing you with his stare and surrounded by the Inventions of Man, from fire to electricity. Around 1900, the operative verb became *commanded*. About that same time, I've learned at the library, the nebulous group of Prophets had devolved to one Veiled Prophet, though the invitation still attested "By Order of G. O." or Grand Oracle.

The costs of each year's invitations alone must have been staggering. Moreover, I recall, as I tuck the last of the relics back into their archival wrapping, each arrived with a token of the Prophet's esteem. My parents left these ashtrays and carafes around the house. The unmistakable scroll of "VP" in the design advertised my father's membership in the club without breaking his oath to secrecy.

Granted, things took a steep downward turn in 1972. The invitation, which my mom preserved along with the others, resembles a wedding announcement, rectangular and white. I remember that the gift was neither crystal nor silver, but *plastic*—a white plastic paperweight and pen from which the "VP" chipped with the flick of a fingernail. It was a lousy gift, everyone agreed, and unfair to us girls, and what the world was coming to with trashy gifts like this, no one could predict.

※　　※　　※

Echoing a wave of sentiment among supporters of the ball, my mother used to liken the event to a party. "You invite your friends," she said. "You can't invite everybody. Then you do the city a big favor by having a lovely parade where people on floats throw candy to children watching. Everybody can come to that. What a generous thing! Nobody ever said to the committee, 'You have to hold a parade, or you can't have your ball.' They pay for the ball, and they can invite or not invite whomever they choose. That's why we live in a democracy."

"But I'll be invited to the ball," I said, sometime around the seventh grade. "And those men on the committee—they don't know me."

"They know your father, and your father knows you."

"That's not the same thing. I could be an awful person."

"They're not electing you to office, honey! They're throwing a party. They're choosing a Queen."

"They're going to pick Hope Jones, from my class," I said.

"You don't know that."

"Everyone says."

"They might choose Ann Mallinckrodt. The Mallinckrodts are very prominent."

"Uh-uh. It'll be Hopie."

"Well, she's a nice girl."

"But why should they choose her? It's not like she's the prettiest."

"Would you want them to choose a girl just because she's pretty?"

This question flummoxed me, but only for a moment. "It's called the Queen of Love and Beauty," I said when I had my bearings.

"That's an expression." My mother cut a glance at me. We talked, most often, in the living room, where she settled into her olive green leather armchair, with its rectangular cushion that went *poossh* when you sat on it. While we talked she knitted or did needle-point. We all wore her sweaters proudly, even if the others at our private schools laughed at their bulkiness and complicated nubs. Later I would grow cruel about my mother's handiwork, which was by all accounts perfection, her stitches small and even and her designs elegant originals or clever knockoffs. But mostly I admired her talents, none of which I shared, enough to overcome my shame at possessing a mother who created things with her hands. "It is an expression," she went on, "you could apply to any of the girls. You're all young. You're all healthy."

"I bet the girls who don't get invited think that, too," I said.

"But it is not their party. Let them have their own party, if they like, and not invite *you*."

"What," I asked at least once, perched on the armrest of her chair, "if I don't want to go?"

"You'll want to go! All your friends will be going!"

I considered myself friendless, but that was beside the point. "What if I don't, when the time comes?"

"Then you won't go. You'll miss out."

My mother pulled extra yarn from the skein. She shook the sweater arm she was knitting and frowned at it as if it had misbe-haved. Because of her knitting, she once told me, they had changed the rules at Washington University, forbidding all students to do handicrafts during lectures. She'd had to sit with nothing but a pen in her hand. My mother earned a degree in business. Until she met my father, she lived at home with her widowed mother and worked for a living. That she had not been a Maid at the ball was a piece of history we all took for granted. Although her mother's family had been prominent enough to gain invitations to the early balls, her father had been second-generation Irish. She had graduated from University City High School. My father's sisters had both attended Mary Institute. Of the eighty-eight Veiled Prophet Queens crowned up to 1972, eighty-three had attended Mary Institute. This fact, I also took for granted, was the main reason I had been sent there.

Seven

The Motions

Watch over our school, O Lord,
As its years increase,
And bless and guide her daughters,
Wherever they may be
Keeping them ever unspotted from the world.

— MARY INSTITUTE'S "PRAYER FOR THE GRADUATES," CIRCA 1972

In 1963, the year I was sent to Mary Institute, Clayton's public schools, in which I had been enrolled, were ranked among the best in the nation. Post-Sputnik dollars were pouring into the nation's public education system; therefore there was no appreciable difference in class size between St. Louis's public and private schools, and the facilities at Mary Institute seemed shabby in comparison to the gleaming new resources at my old school. I had already learned most of the math facts and language skills Miss Purcell was teaching to the fourth graders at Mary Institute, so at year's end I was promoted to sixth grade. Clearly, academics had nothing to do with my being placed in Mary Institute.

On the other hand, *Brown v. Board of Education* had been decided. At the public high school, they were grinding their hips to Elvis. Jazz and reefers were out of the box and in the news. The white-pillared walls of a girls' private school looked safe; or safer, anyway. Moreover, the adults my parents knew or wanted to know were all sitting in the parents' meetings at Mary Institute and its brother school, St. Louis Country Day. You want to be, as my mother kept reminding me, where your friends are. Most of life, it seemed, had to do with remaining among your friends.

I do not know that we at Mary Institute remained unspotted. We did learn, in Upper School dance class, to bow to the floor and rise again without our hips wobbling or our knees cracking. Sallie Estep, who sat in front of me in study hall, learned more. Although her chest, in everyone's view, was too developed for a ballerina, she spent a summer studying with Martha Graham and returned to do a provocative solo on the chapel stage. She also returned with boy-short hair and a penchant for Angela Davis. She set up a rack outside the Senior Room and sold all her clothes except one plain black dress, which she washed daily and wore until it shredded at the seams; then she bought a brown dress and did the same with that. I bought one of Sallie's blouses, an ivory lacy thing with a scalloped neckline that my mother told me exposed my unsightly collarbone.

The rest of us learned just enough in dance class to do our bows at the annual May Day Fête and later at the Veiled Prophet Ball. Then we tried out for field hockey.

Throughout my years at Mary Institute, I operated with the illusion that my *commadres* were, like me, going through the motions. Life as I understood it lay where Sallie Estep had briefly gone—somewhere outside and beyond. Our attendance at Junior League dancing lessons, our allegiance to certain brands of clothing, and our acquiescence to the rituals of "coming out" amounted to a role we performed for the benefit of our elders. We enacted this role with a wink toward one another. We would discard it as we attained our majority and the revolution commenced.

Imagine, then, my surprise in 1972.

⌖   ⌖   ⌖

When he arrived in St. Louis, Michael Edson's hair straggled midway down his back. His beard, while scruffy, was long enough to require extensive combing, which he did as a nervous habit, with a black pocket comb missing a few of its teeth. He held onto his vowels in a druggy variation on the popular pot-laced humor of Cheech and Chong. He gestured rapidly with his hands as he spoke, always with the fingers splayed as if holding onto a teacup.

"Has your hair always been this long?" my mother asked when we had completed a round of introductions.

"Oh no!" said Michael. He stood in front of our hall mirror, combing his beard. "When I was in Switzerland with the Maharishi," he said, "it was almost a foot longer."

He winked at me. I felt, simultaneously, the sensations of perfect success and utter failure. Success because Michael embodied nearly everything of which my parents would disapprove without just cause. Failure because one look at my mother convinced me that whatever her faults, she did not deserve such an ungrateful, stubborn, and stupid daughter as I had turned out to be.

The afternoon of Michael's arrival, we rented tails for the ball. "How do I look?" he said, smiling almost sweetly as he turned before the tuxedo store's three-way mirror.

"Russian," I said.

"Rasputin?" he tried.

"I guess," I said. I was busy marveling at how a well-cut tailcoat could make even Michael Edson appear attractive. He looked taller than usual, his beard was combed, and the jacket padded his shoulders nicely.

"I'm going to introduce myself to everyone here as Michael Romanov," he said. "Romanov," he repeated, rolling the R.

"They'll still know you're Jewish," I said.

"But I'll be a white Russian Jew," he said, combing his beard before the full-length mirror in the store.

"Are there such people?" I said.

"No," he said. "That's the fun of it."

That night we attended a debutante party, I no longer recall whose, at the Missouri Bar Association.

I had been to several of these, the previous summer, with varying degrees of lavish outlay. The most spectacular had been Ann Mallinckrodt's. An heiress to the fortune of Mallinckrodt Chemical Corporation, Ann had not even applied to college. While the rest of us were losing our collective virginity to one track athlete or another, she was renting her own flat in London. For her homecoming party, the 1904 St. Louis World's Fair was re-created in the backyard of her father's home on McKnight Place, with various booths for entertainment and music by members of Jefferson Airplane. Guests were encouraged to attend in costume, and I had made myself a flounced skirt split up the front, with a lacy leotard underneath. There had been cancan girls, I reasoned, at the World's Fair; there had been cancan girls in France, and St. Louis was a French town. As with my reaction to Michael's appearance in our front hall, I was at once proud of myself and embarrassed by my relatively scanty attire—the other debs came to the party not as showgirls but as women of the era, in long skirts with bustles and Gibson girl hairdos. The young men made a gesture of dressing up, with a top hat or suspenders, but mostly they attended as the props on which the women hung their wares.

I danced a lot at Ann Mallinckrodt's party. The more I danced, the happier I was to be a cancan girl. I felt pretty. I felt California. I felt slightly slutty. I felt like a visitor to the rich, humid air of the Midwest, like one to whom the rules needn't apply.

There were other parties, most of them exercises in alcohol tolerance. My brother Dan attended more than I, as it was considered etiquette to have more men than women. He never drank himself into a stupor, like the boy who threw up on me at Kathy Fordyce's party. He loved the professionalism, if I can call it that, of these affairs—the sense that he qualified for attendance, for the clubby jokes by the bar and the group memories of similar parties, of long drunken drives into the country or skinny dips in the country club pool before dawn.

"Your brother is perfect," Michael Edson said as Dan dropped us off in front of the bar association. We both laughed, low and catty. I was ashamed of myself—but as Michael and I wove our way through the perfumed crowd at the Missouri Bar Association, I thought it was all sort of a joke, my brother included, and we were the jokesters. I hung on Michael's arm as if he were really my lover and not my rival in love. Everyone was smoking cigarettes. Girls within reach of blond had frosted their hair and cropped it to their shoulders. No one had any skin problems, anymore. As they spotted me, they pointed their cigarettes at me and scrunched their faces into what might have been the beginning of a laugh. "Lulu Belle!"

I remember several shouting at me, as if that had been my nick-name in some forgotten southern corner of my past. I introduced Michael.

"Romanov," he said. His hand hung limply in theirs. They smirked at me as if he were a catch—a poor catch, but one on which they were prepared to congratulate me. I did my best to look blank.

We drank gin and tonics at the bar. Michael was chatty and oblivious, smoking cigarettes, gesturing with his hands. He was, I believe, discoursing on the bombing of Haiphong Harbor, an issue that the Nixon administration had avoided up to the moment of its election the month before. "McGovern *told* everybody," I remember his saying. "That's what you get for speaking the *truth* in this *country*."

A man my father's age turned abruptly from a more amiable conversation. He looked Michael up and down. Then he reached over to grab hold of the silver coke spoon Michael was wearing around his neck, over his tie. He glared. "What is this thing?" he asked.

"That, sir," said Michael without missing a beat, "is an antique tiki god."

The man stared hard at the spoon, then back at Michael, then looked at the spoon again. I thought he had probably had too many martinis. He let the spoon drop back on Michael's tie, and he held out his hand. "Fred Schlafly," he said in a tone of noble defeat.

"Michael Romanov," said Michael. "Glad to meet you."

I exhaled. Gently I led Michael away. "You should be careful who you talk to that way," I said.

"Hey, he loved me," said Michael.

"The Schlaflys are very big in St. Louis. You ever hear of Phyllis Schlafly?"

"Most of these people would be happier if they learned to meditate," said Michael.

As I had when dressed as a cancan girl, I believed my exotic accoutrement—in this case, Michael Romanov—gave me access to the other girls that I had heretofore lacked. I made this mistake because I assumed a general shift toward the logic of forbidden things and away from the absurd life for which we had been trained. So when one of the frosted young women bent politely toward me and said, "So who's your boyfriend, Lulu Belle?" I said with borrowed timing, "Oh. My *boyfriend*. Right." I expected her to laugh. She did not. She looked puzzled. I believe I then asked her if she thought there would be any action at the ball.

"Action?" she said. She took a sip of her drink, a lime green concoction in a crystal tumbler.

"You know. The Black Panthers or whatever. Something to wake the party up."

"Oh, that." She rolled her blue eyes. Eyes were very blue, that year—tinted contacts had just come in, and shadow was applied above and below the eyes, giving pretty young women that bruised look. "People don't know any better, I guess," she said.

"Sure they do." I'd had too much to drink. I plowed straight ahead. "They're going to bring this racist thing down. I can't wait. Do you have any idea how much this shit costs?" I waved my arm to indicate the chandeliers, the bar with its demure black bartenders, and the band sawing away on a raised platform at the end of the room. "Children are starving in Cambodia," I said.

"Sure, I got it," said Frosted. "I'll eat up all my peas."

I wasn't doing well. I knew I wasn't doing well, but I was beginning to lose my bearings. When Michael Romanov came over, waggling his antique tiki god, I was almost grateful to him, to his blithe willingness, his having no stake in this matter.

⌗   ⌗   ⌗

Back at my mother's house on Maryhill Lane, a narrow bed was made up for Michael in the closet-size study. I had my own room, though not one I had ever lived in when I lived at home. I hung my party dress in a closet with a sliding door, next to the hanging bags in which my mother kept out-of-season suits and dresses. Some of my old furniture was in the room; some of it had been sold or stored. I knew my mother and sister lived in this house, but everything about it felt temporary to me.

That night I slept lightly and nervously, and I worried mostly that Michael would think he ought to sneak into my room and make a pass at me. Lying in bed, I missed things in turns. My cat Socrates, who had slept with me in my dorm room back in California. My dorm room itself, with its odor of new paint and the bougainvillea outside the window. My old cat, who had slept with me as I grew up, and who had escaped from this house to run down the weedy hill onto Ladue Road, where she was killed by a car. The room I had grown up in, back in Clayton, with its window that gave onto the front porch roof, where I could sneak out at night and meditate under the stars. My father and mother, sleeping on the other side of the connecting bathroom in that house, their peevishness soothed by slumber.

And then I woke, and it was the day of the ball. Michael was slouching in my doorway, in a brownish Indian robe, grinning behind his beard. "I've got it," he said.

"Got what?" I said.

"We can make brownies. You know, with grass. You know how to make brownies, right?"

"Sure," I said. I squinted at him; the light through the window was bright. Snow had fallen during the night.

"They will put you in the mood," Michael said.

"Okay," I said.

"We can eat a couple before you go down to the place, and you can pack a couple to eat later. It'll be great."

"My mom'll know we made brownies, though. She'll want to taste them."

As soon as I said this I felt panic knot my stomach. Feeding one's mother Alice B. Toklas brownies had to be the sine qua non of prankster activity. It was the sort of stunt you read about in underground comics. The mothers loosened up and had sex; the children, slightly horrified, locked up the rest of their stash.

"Far out," said Michael.

"No, really. It wouldn't be cool. She'd hate the taste. She'd know before she even got high." I had never eaten dope brownies before, but these facts seemed unassailable to me.

"So we'll air out the kitchen. You want to be high when you're doing this thing, don't you?"

"For sure," I said. I liked getting high, as Michael knew. I liked the way time slowed down when I smoked, and the way my mental processes seemed to roll on top of a sturdy bubble. In fact, I had not thought of making my debut on a marijuana high, but now that Michael had mentioned it, there seemed no other way to get through the evening than on the slow magic carpet of cannabis. "We can say," I tried, swinging my legs over the side of my bed, "we took them over to my friend Emily's house."

"Far out," said Michael. He stepped into the room and up to the bed. He leaned his thighs into my knees. I breathed in the cheese-like odor of his crotch. My mother had gone to work; my brother slept in the one-room carriage house in the backyard; and my sister had spent the night with a friend.

"You don't really want anything like this," I said to Michael's belt buckle.

"We could try it," he said.

I was wearing the unsexiest thing I owned, a flowered Lanz flannel gown. I pictured flinging it off, standing on the bed in my young naked glory, and telling Michael Edson to take me. My mouth twisted. "Oh, please," I said.

"Maybe when you're high," said Michael. "Women get really horny when they're high."

"I get sleepy," I said.

"You just don't get high enough. First you're sleepy, then you're horny. We'll eat the brownies. You'll see."

⌗   ⌗   ⌗

We made them, that afternoon, from scratch, melting the dark squares of chocolate, whisking in the bright yellow margarine. I ate two and Michael ate three, then we wrapped up some to cram into my pocketbook and into his coat pocket. It was snowing outside, the wet heavy flakes of the lower Midwest. We opened all the windows and ran the blower over the stove on high. Then Michael went for a walk in the mushy stuff while I took a shower and began the methodical process of getting ready: hair, nails, face. For a long while I didn't feel high at all, just bitter in the mouth from the brown leaves mixed into the batter. I rolled my hair onto blue Velcro tubes. Just as I was beginning to float, to curl my thoughts around the bubble, the backdoor opened and my mother's voice sang out. "Baking brownies?"

"We took them over to Emily's!" I shouted.

"Too bad!" she said. "Smells good!"

I rolled the long locks of my hair. Guilt was a by-product, disposable. We were on our way.

Eight

Founding Fathers

They did not know who the Veiled Prophets were—
and who does?—but they had a guarantee that
something GRAND and WEIRD was to occur.

— *MISSOURI REPUBLICAN*, October 9, 1878

When I follow the thread of the Veiled Prophet Ball back to the myth that gave it its name, I find rape, murder, and battle. When I follow the thread back to the ball's origins as a marriage market, I find power brokers and land seizures. When I follow it back to the ball's origins in St. Louis, I find a labor dispute.

I'm thinking about such beginnings as I wend my way across Missouri on Interstate 70, listening to a tape of Jane Smiley's novel *A Thousand Acres.* Three hours takes me to Kansas City, then another hour north to Maryville, home of Northwest Missouri State University and the author of the only book-length study of the Veiled Prophet Ball.

I discovered Thomas Spencer by doing a keyword search for articles featuring the words *Veiled* and *Prophet* in any combination. There were, needless to say, few articles that contained both terms, and the rest had nothing to do with the St. Louis ball. Spencer's article, "Power on Parade," appeared in *Gateway Heritage,* the journal of the Missouri Historical Society. When I contacted him, three months before, he eagerly sent me the book-length manuscript, "The Origins and History of the Veiled Prophet Celebration

in St. Louis, 1877-1995," which he had just defended as his disser-
tation for Indiana University.

Several of the people I've interviewed in St. Louis also spoke to
Tom Spencer, though they didn't like him much. He struck them
as an outsider, asking rote questions. But his careful accumulation
of historical evidence has connected, for me, a series of dots from
the dread Mokanna to the slender Santa Claus.

Had anyone asked why I was going to Maryville, I would have
said I was doing research. But there remains little Tom Spencer can
tell me that his book has not divulged. The fact is that I am driving
simply to meet this young man who has drawn such sharp outlines
from the murky past.

I pass the low hills above the Ozarks, driving through the last
vestiges of damp air before I hit the hundredth meridian. In a
snowless January, the land looks scraped bare. Missouri is tied with
Tennessee for having the most other states touching its borders. I
discovered this fact during an idle moment in fourth-grade geog-
raphy and have never forgotten it. Multiple borders and crossings
inexorably link and define my home state. To the people with
whom I attended college in California, Missouri—and especially
St. Louis—is "back East." To my neighbors in Connecticut, it is
"out West." To Dixie southerners, it will always seem northern; to
abolitionist northerners, southern. From St. Louis, it seems, you can
go anywhere. Scott Joplin did, and T. S. Eliot; Chuck Berry,
Ntozake Shange, Kate Chopin, Mark Twain, Sara Teasdale, Maya
Angelou, Tennessee Williams, Miles Davis, Dick Gregory, Harold
Brodkey, William S. Burroughs, all of these people and more sprang
from here to seek their fortunes. Didn't Lewis and Clark choose St.
Louis as their jumping-off point? Wasn't the first flight to Paris
made in the *Spirit of St. Louis* and the first balloon flight around the
globe navigated by a St. Louisan?

Yet it is that very malleable, externally derived character that
makes St. Louis an ideal place to be from—an ideal place, that is,
to leave. One can adapt oneself to other parts of America because
there is always a wisp of St. Louis in every place where one might
settle. And one can exchange identities—Southern California, for
instance, for New England, where I now live—simply by trading

in one set of St. Louis assumptions for another. Being able to live anywhere you choose is another way of saying that you come from nowhere, or everywhere.

Tom Spencer lives with his pregnant wife and his toddler in an overly furnished house on a gray street in a university town. He is a tall, soft young man who is concerned mostly with his prospects for tenure. We take a walk to the center of town for coffee. "I was surprised, really," he says, "that the historical society would even print the article. I toned it down a little, so maybe they didn't quite get what I was saying."

"And what were you saying?" I ask.

"That those men screwed up the city of St. Louis," Tom Spencer says calmly.

"Where are you from originally?"

"North Little Rock, Arkansas. I didn't know anything about the Veiled Prophet until I studied a year at Mizzou."

"Strange tradition, huh?"

"Yeah!" He rolls his eyes and chuckles. "I don't think it was a good subject to choose, though," he says, shaking his narrow head. "No one in Missouri wants to publish the book, that's for sure. And with another little one coming . . . ." He glances anxiously in the direction of his house. "It's the only book I've got," he says.

"It's a good book."

He seems to see me for the first time. "Why should you care?" he asks.

"I was there," I tell him. "On the stage, in 1972."

"When did you start thinking about writing about it?"

"On the stage. In 1972."

"But what are you trying to find out?"

I have a hard time meeting his eyes. I feel as if I have suddenly sprouted green antlers. "Where I came from, I guess," I finally say. "What I was doing there."

"Well, it's obvious what you were doing there," Tom Spencer says. "You were preserving the status quo."

He does not mean this as a judgment. He is a young historian after material, and he has stumbled onto the dark truths of my hometown much the way Captain Kirk of the *Enterprise* might stumble onto a malignant life-form on another planet. But part of me wants to protest, as those elongated one-eyed aliens might have protested to the well-meaning captain, *You do not understand us at all.*

Jane Smiley's novel, to which I listen as I retrace the long road back to St. Louis, is a modern reprise of *King Lear.* That is, it tells the story of a powerful father and the daughters who vie for his legacy. I don't much care for Smiley's characters, not even the Cordelia figure, but they wear a face I recognize. That the father might be pigheaded or mad is beside the point, as is the money he has to bestow. The women seek his blessing. When he withholds it, they go sour and mean.

In the summer of 1972, when my father told his friends that his daughter would be presented at the Veiled Prophet Ball that fall, his face was beaming. I had let him down so much, in so many ways. Surely I could give him this. Surely for once I could do the right thing, could be beautiful in the right way, could be Cordelia. And just as surely, I was determined to give him nothing at all.

Perhaps this is what is afoot with me. Perhaps I should have answered Tom Spencer, "I am trying to find out if my father loved me. If what lay behind the mess and the greed, however much we may posture and condemn, was love."

By "me" I don't mean me personally. I mean all of us, the fathers too. Though the quest remains personal, of course.

⌘   ⌘   ⌘

The next morning I'm back at the Missouri Historical Society on Skinker Boulevard, across from Forest Park. Once seen as the perimeter of civilization in St. Louis, the park is now a place for caution after dark. I follow the paper trail that Tom Spencer has mapped. When I need air, I cross the boulevard and stride up the spongy turf of the city golf course to Museum Hill, where we used to sled and where the weak sun beats down on the statue of Saint Louis astride his horse.

In my earliest memory, the high-prancing steed and its crowned rider are the symbol of the city, the French saint's grave features blending with the somewhat bereaved wisdom of the Veiled Prophet. Later, a committee will deem the statue of Saint Louis too

Old-World a symbol and substitute a tricolor map of the convergence of the Ohio, Missouri, and Mississippi rivers to denote St. Louis's future as the place where commerce meets. This notion has lead-balloon appeal and soon gives way to the Arch, the Gateway to the West. But I miss the personal appeal of the noble king, his scepter held aloft, his spine erect, his horse's right hoof obediently lifted. Whatever his symbolic weaknesses, he has the founding-father look down pat.

From the historical society, I drive out to my father's house for lunch. My father and Nancy live just over the border from Clayton into Ladue, in an umbral house with family portraits and framed documents on the walls. As I pull into the driveway I'm thinking about Mary Ambrose Smith, the pale, dark-haired woman who was Veiled Prophet Queen in 1928. Her reign was at perhaps the height of cotillion splendor in the Midwest. Although the French saint's city had slipped from being the fourth largest in the nation to being the sixth, and electricity, motor cars, and the movies had taken a toll on the adult audience for parades, the ball had risen steadily in stature to become the grandest social event west of Philadelphia. The stock market was booming. Wealth and female beauty were idolized and celebrated. Over this, Mary Ambrose Smith was to rule.

Unhappily, as I have just discovered, Miss Smith learned of her planned coronation only a few days before the ball itself. She was living in Atlanta at the time and had that very week, in secret, married a young banker. It was against the rules for the Queen to be anything other than a maid—it constituted, if you will, a sort of bigamy—but Mary's siblings warned her that news of her nuptials would "break Father's heart." And so Mary kept her status secret from the prophet organization and from J. Sheppard Smith, who had counted on this moment to enshrine his place in the business world.

I picture her treading the long white carpet, her eyes gleaming, her train flowing behind her, approaching the seated Prophet, as she hopes against hope that she can do her part and be, years later, forgiven.

But like Moore's Zelica, she is doomed. When the truth came

out, a few days after Mary Smith's crowning, the Grand Oracle had her scuttled out of the city, her name blotted from the social register. "Begone, little girl," he told Mary. "Don't register at any large hotels, and don't use your real name." Whether her father forgave her or even saw her again is not known. To this day, Veiled Prophet chronologies list "no Queen" for that year.

My father fixes his own lunch, a bowl of Campbell's soup every day. He takes pride in this homemaking skill. Nancy works—with his approval, he always adds—and is gone from the house all day. I toast whole wheat bread and get the peanut butter out of the fridge. I tell him what I've learned about Mary Ambrose Smith, but he knows the story already. His sister Ann, he points out, learned her lesson from Mary. "At the ball where Ann was Queen, you know," he says, stirring water into condensed beef barley, "all the young men wanted to dance with her, of course. And there was this fellow Joe Harris down from Detroit. He'd just taken a job with Shell Oil. And he danced with Ann more than once, you can rely on that!"

"Uncle Joe," I said.

My father nods. He sticks his pinkie finger into the pot of soup, to test it, then he licks the finger. He dresses in a clean oxford shirt every day, with a cardigan sweater and a nicely buffed pair of wing-tips. When he goes out, he wears a fedora, but he rarely goes out in the winter. He is eighty-eight and believes with almost equal fervor in the divinity of Christ and the miracles of modern medicine. In 1931, when Ann made her debut, he was an undergraduate at Yale, majoring in economics, planning to get this country back on its feet again. Later in the Depression, when his father announced that tuition funds were no longer available, he put himself through law school by creating and then coaching the fencing team at Washington University.

"Ann took the year off from Vassar, of course," he continues at the table when he has said grace, "to attend to her queenly duties. But you know, she became engaged to Joe about a month after the ball."

"I thought you said she learned her lesson from Mary Smith," I say.

"She did." He dips his head, scoops soup, and wipes his chin with a paper napkin.

"Well, then, how did she keep her crown? Mary Smith got deported."

My father puts the back of his hand to his pursed mouth, as if he's still keeping the secret. "We didn't *tell*," he says. A fleck of barley erupts from his mouth. His thin lips tremble. "That's what saved her!" Breaking into a long-toothed grin, he cuts a wedge of cheese to go with the soup.

In October 1932, the day after Ann turned over her crown to the next lucky girl, she announced her betrothal. A few weeks later she married Joe, opening the door to the rest of her life. "Like a fairy tale," I say to my father.

My father and I do not discuss what he and I both know. Joe Harris was Jewish. After leaving his father, Harmon, his mother brought him up in Switzerland, and when he returned to the States, he passed as Gentile. Joe and Ann attended the Episcopal church in St. Louis and later in Mystic, Connecticut. Their children learned their father's secret only after they were grown, and only from Joe's sister; neither he nor Ann ever told them of their Jewish heritage. Joe was buried in the Ferriss family plot. After Ann's death a few years ago, her children sent my father a letter sharing their knowledge and looking for more answers. "The response," my cousin has written me, "was silence."

⚖ ⚖ ⚖

The story of the Veiled Prophet is a cotillion story, a myth, a civil rights story, and a gender tale—but it is also a story of St. Louis. And St. Louis's bookends, I realize after lunching with my father, are New Orleans and Chicago. For if St. Louis is neither northern nor southern, eastern nor western, then Chicago is northeastern, New Orleans southwestern. Following Tom Spencer's manuscript once again to the archives of the Missouri Historical Society, I find the bridge linking these three cities in the strike of 1877 and in the story of one Colonel Alonzo Slayback, of the Confederate Army.

In the early 1870s, when Colonel Slayback removed from New Orleans to St. Louis, the rivalry between St. Louis and Chicago for industrial preeminence in America's heartland was furious. In terms of population, Chicago was still third after New York and Philadelphia, but St. Louis could claim a more temperate climate and the frontier energy for which it was known. Moreover, the men of power Slayback found in Lafayette's landlocked city counted on the great St. Louis Agricultural and Mechanical Fair to draw rich farmers and investors to the city and proclaim it as a hub of commerce.

But in the middle of that decade, a series of labor slowdowns led to the workers' strike of 1877 and brought America's fourth largest city to its knees. During one hot July week, St. Louis manufactures came to a standstill. A citizens' militia brought out bayonets to end the action, but the seeds of unrest had been planted and were ready to sprout the following year.

The men who ran St. Louis considered themselves visionaries. The coopers, molders, and mechanics opposing their benevolent dictatorship, it stood to reason, were blind. The unrest they might cause at the 1878 agricultural and mechanical fair, on which the city's business and industry depended, would prove disastrous. A symbol had to be found; one that would embody the wisdom of the elite and lift St. Louis—and its inner circle—to safe prosperity.

Fortunately, Slayback had discovered the perfect icon, in New Orleans. Inviting twenty businessmen to "attend a meeting of prominent gentlemen," Slayback proposed for the 1878 fair a pageant-style show of power based on a New Orleans Carnival float depicting a romantic "Veiled Prophet" taken from the wildly popular *Lalla Rookh*. This exotic figure was to "be recognized as infallible" and would serve as both inspiration and warning to the rabble. Great rumors of his coming were circulated, wild speculation encouraged, and a grand parade foretold.

The first image of the Veiled Prophet that ever appeared, in the *Missouri Republican* (in which Slayback conveniently held a controlling interest), depicted a Klanish figure with black hollows for eyes and double-barreled pistols in both hands, a supernatural vigilante. "He will not likely be stopped by street cars or anything else," the newspaper warned. Indeed, as the Prophet arrived by barge, fast behind the impressive *Robert E. Lee* riverboat, the crowds parted respectfully; they allowed power to pass.

"By having a parade every year that showed a make-believe mideast king and his court," Tom Spencer wrote, "the St. Louis elite asserted the value of social hierarchy both in the mythical kingdom of Khorassan and in the real world of St. Louis. The fact that it was organized by the same people who had organized the citizens' militia, and that only the elite were invited to join, made clear the outlines of that hierarchy." Membership in the organization, Spencer noted, cost one hundred dollars in its first year, about one-sixth of an average workingman's salary.

Here was something the helter-skelter metropolis of Chicago lacked. Chicago's parades were shows of mere populism. Its ruling class had force but not fraternity, and its people could not look, as St. Louisans now could, to a stout group of patriarchs to lead them in civility as well as enterprise. Above all, Chicago lacked charm.

Early descriptions of the Veiled Prophet are laced with a frat-boy humor and an in-group chumminess. There were ironic gibes at one another, as when the *Missouri Republican*, run by the Veiled Prophet Society, published hasty drawings of the mysterious visitor that it claimed "the *Republican,* with a complete abandon as regards expense, has had engraved." There were painful puns, as in the cartoon caption of the Prophet and "Krewe" flying away in a seashell-like contraption: "They will disappear in an airship. The above is that 'are [that there] ship." Glib satire laces the news report. "Wealth," claimed the *Republican* in the middle of the first "rumors" of the parade in 1878, "is not visible to the naked eye, because it has gradually all gone into the statesman's pocket."

I recognize this mix of arrogance and self-deprecation. It's typical of the long-winded jokes my uncles used to tell and laugh at halfway through the punch line. Their wives would grimace and say, "Oh, you're bad." The men never meant anything, did they, by such charming frivolities, or the pranks that went along with them? Wasn't the teller making himself out, half the time, to be the biggest dunce of all?

The feminist lightbulb joke goes like this. Question: "How many feminists does it take to screw in a lightbulb?" Answer: "That's not funny."

In other words, reading the early, madcap humor about the

Veiled Prophet, I am both unamused and guilty for being unamused, as if whoever is not laughing will be the butt of the next joke. I have to remind myself that I laugh at other jokes from the nineteenth century; that I love Mark Twain. I howled at *Tristram Shandy.* I am not altogether a blue stocking stuck in the mud.

The point, in any case, is that the founding fathers of St. Louis found the jokes funny, and they held the parade with the pistol-wielding Prophet, and the strike of 1878 never went off. And so they held the parade again the next year, and the next. The crowds of three hundred thousand and more that lined the parade route didn't find it funny. They remained, in fact, peculiarly silent—"hedges of humanity," according to the *Missouri Republican,* "almost as mute as the costumed figures in the tableaux." Still, they watched.

Each float in the parade got a full paragraph, each year, in the newspaper. Some were floats of progress, splendid floats illuminated by gas and then by electricity, spreading their light over the city. Others were floats of the funny drunken Irish mine workers; of the funny darkies on the ol' plantation; and of the funny Indian chiefs in their funny death throes. Women on the floats were usually funny because they were men dressed up. Pocahontas warranted an exception because she was a girl, and she helped John Smith. Also unfunny, in the float bringing up the rear of the parade, was the big statue of a busty woman who represented truth or freedom. The original of this carved heroine, in the 1878 parade, got to sit on top of a mountain of mineral mines, with baskets of produce all around. *Plenty,* they called her, and her message was that if the amusing men who'd made the floats stayed in charge, the city and the state—yea, the whole nation—would prosper.

Occasionally, the joker's arrogance caught up with him. Two of the original Veiled Prophet founders, Alonzo Slayback and J. C. Normile, got bit by their own antics. Slayback's turn came first, in 1882, after the parade had proved a huge success and the ball a self-congratulating bacchanalia. The *St. Louis Post-Dispatch*—consolidated and revitalized by Joseph Pulitzer the same year the Veiled Prophet celebrations began—had printed some disparaging remarks about Slayback's law partner. Slayback, incensed, publicly accused the paper's editors of being "a gang of blackmailers." With

Joe Pulitzer away in New York, John Cockerill, the managing editor, responded in the *Post-Dispatch* to Slayback's accusation by quoting charges that Slayback was a "coward and a blowhard." That afternoon a heavily armed Slayback charged into Cockerill's office, and in the ensuing altercation, Cockerill shot and killed Slayback.

According to a history of the time, "It was a clear case of self defense," and Cockerill was never indicted. Nonetheless, the city and state divided into armed camps that echoed the recent division of the Civil War. Police dispersed a lynch mob gathered in front of the *Post-Dispatch,* bloodthirsty for Cockerill. The two sides were reconciled only when Pulitzer hired Colonel Slayback's second daughter, the sister of the first Veiled Prophet's Belle of the Ball, to be society editor of the *Post-Dispatch.* She remained on the payroll, like Faulkner's Miss Emily, for the rest of her life.

I can't bring myself to dislike Slayback, any more than I could bring myself to dislike Rhett Butler in *Gone with the Wind* or Basil Ransom wreaking havoc in *The Bostonians.* He was a big man, a "southern sizzler" according to reports, finely dressed in clothes brought north from New Orleans. In the photos I find of him at the historical society, he has a jaunty tilt to his head, a bristly mustache, and sleepy, cocksure eyes. Like my uncles—and, noticeably, unlike my father—he seems charming and incorrigible, a man of large passions, large ignorance, and large mistakes. No wonder, I think, they owed his daughter something for the loss of her dad.

Judge J. C. Normile's story is even sadder. Four years after Slayback's death, the *Post-Dispatch* criticized Normile, another self-deprecating Veiled Prophet founder who claimed a line of southern aristocracy. The paper called him "a bump on a log," and Normile sued for libel. On the first day of the trial, the attorney for the *Post-Dispatch* asked Normile a routine question: "Where were you born?" Normile excused himself from the witness stand, went home, and put a bullet through his head.

Now here, I think, is a mystery—but I need not dig much further for the solution. Normile wasn't a bump on a log. He was, a later bulletin reports, "the able and ambitious son of Irish immigrants." Like others in the Veiled Prophet organization, he had invented an aristocratic lineage, complete with a southern plantation where he had first seen the world. If he had answered the bailiff's question truthfully under oath, he would have revealed the fantasy of his past. The prophets were supposed to be infallible—that was the whole point. If you couldn't be infallible you might as well be dead.

If you *were* infallible, on the other hand, you could choose a moment, two or three even, of expensive silliness. The men in the Veiled Prophet organization could *choose* to play dress up and to have a secret language. They could prance around with the pomposity of the Bengal Lancers and tout the gossamer "wisdom" of the "prophet." But to be silly by accident was a cardinal sin.

What pressure, I think. Infallibility! My own father had none of the wit but all of the righteousness. His choler invariably rose at the suggestion that he might have erred. He drove the car with both feet—right foot for gas, left for brake. Although we went through brake pads with astonishing speed, my father could not admit he rode the brake with his left foot. "But when you're not braking, Dad," my persistent sister once asked at dinner, "where *is* your left foot?"

"On the floor!" my father cried out—and throwing down his napkin, he flung himself out of the room.

Infallibility is not the same as perfection, of course. It has to do only with judgment, with the inability to choose wrongly or speak falsely. Lear's doom was his fallible judgment of his own daughters. For the founding fathers of St. Louis, the very choice of their city bore witness to their infallibility. Midway between New Orleans, that sick heart of the South, and Chicago, with its absence of grace, St. Louis promised a sort of perfect marriage—between commerce and art, prosperity and adventure, north and south, east and west. Likewise, the Belle of the Ball blossomed quickly into the Prophet's publicly lauded, infallibly chosen Queen—who was herself, as we lesser daughters strove to be, unspotted and without taint.

Nine

Television

*Wide-eyed and wondering, the ranks of faces of
every hue and nation which enter into the
population of the city are raised with like degree
of interest when the Veiled Prophet passes.*

— WALTER B. STEVENS, *St. Louis, The Fourth City,* 1909

T he lack of taint is public. That is the point. I don't mean the
accusations and defenses of the Prophets' infallibility,
though they were public as well, of course. I mean the girls'
lack of taint.

As my mother drove me down the slick snow-battered streets,
past the high checkered windows of Union Station and the
buttressed cathedral, past the warehouses and into the crowded
alleyways around Kiel Auditorium, I felt for the first time in my life
like a public figure. Protesters lined the streets, their placards and
banners held high. Someone was barking instructions through a
megaphone. A police cordon waved us through, the cars' headlights
blinking like a Christmas commercial. One tall young black man
leaped in front of our Pinto, his sign reading "KKK=VP." "What
do you think of your comrades now?" my mother asked politely as
we inched our way around to the back of the stadium.

"They have a right," I said. I twisted in the seat to get a better
glimpse as the tall man receded from the car.

"They need something better to occupy their time," my mother
said.

I had heard that somewhere before. Hadn't I? I was really stoned by now; words slipped in and out of their envelopes. Oh, yes. I had said it myself—written it, to Percy Green. I had told him that we were killing people in Southeast Asia, as if this was news. Who was Percy Green? Was he out there, somewhere, one of the dark faces, made larger by a snow-frosted Afro, moving in and out of the curtain of falling white? I had participated in only one traffic-stopping protest, with Peace Action. We had lain down across the San Bernardino Freeway about thirty miles outside Los Angeles during the morning rush hour, while our buddies stuck antiwar leaflets underneath stalled commuters' windshields. After twenty minutes and two traffic holdups, I withdrew to the shoulder of the road. "I can't do this any more," I said to one of my fellow protesters, an economics major hoisting a large sign that accused Richard Nixon of genocide.

"Why not?" he said.

"We're not converting anybody to the cause. They're just pissed off at us."

"Sometimes being pissed off is the only way a person starts thinking," he said.

"Well, I can't do it any more."

He drew back. Through round wire-rimmed glasses he looked at me. "This is the first time," he said, "that I've ever seen you out of your element."

I took his remark as a compliment. My element was wide. It was wide and nondiscriminating. It wasn't the San Bernardino Freeway at rush hour, maybe, but it encompassed most everything else. I rose to occasions. I knew how to handle myself.

Only this, too—this car parking at the back entrance of Keil Auditorium, my door being opened by a courteous black attendant with a large black umbrella and white gloves to lead me from my seat—was also my element. And for what had the elite daughters of the South been bred, if not to handle themselves well in any element? To hold their milky-white necks erect while crude Union soldiers burned their homes and roasted their pigs and left them in a shanty with nothing but cornmeal and slaves to be fed?

※　　※　　※

I say *South* because I am looking now, years after the ball, at St. Louis in its incarnation as the northwest outpost of the expired Confederacy. I say *South* because the element in which I swam, exiting the shell-blue Pinto into the gracious humility of the door-man's umbrella, once represented a break with the tradition of coming out, and the rupture was pecularily southern. I say *South* because the daughters of the antebellum South were the first to witness this ritual's eruption from private to public sphere.

⚜   ⚜   ⚜

Once upon a time in England, you were presented to the queen. (Notice there's no active voice here. Ideally, your guardians presented you as they would an ornate piece of crystal, off which the light sparkles without any conscious choice on the crystal's part. There's something seductive about getting presented in this way. If it all goes wrong, who can blame you? No crystal ever cut its own bevels.) The royal court's annual move to London, which was followed by a wave of presentations, opened the "season." The season involved hunting, horse racing, and parties. Country gentry also moved to town and went to marketing their daughters—"often with the hope," writes the British historian Margaret Pringle, "that perhaps some double marriage treaty could involve a swop of daughters and property to the benefit of both families." As Countess Zamoyska, who was orig-inally from unexotic Devon, put it,

> The season had started with those people who were rich enough and important enough to own a London house, which they occupied at certain times of the year according to the English sporting calendar—that is, the only times when the men could be persuaded to come to London. This meant the mating season of the pheasant, the fox, the partridge and the grouse. . . . There were no Jews, or very few. . . . You only entertained in your own home. Unless you had a house large enough for a ball, you could not have a party so you could not go to parties.

(*There were no Jews.* Witness Michael Edson, Semitic, fresh from the shower in my mother's house while I stepped across the clogged gutter to the sidewalk at the back of Kiel Auditorium. I knew the taboo we were breaking. When I was five years old, my best friend was a boy named Mark Heimann. He lived around the corner, had a round face framed by dark curls, and was the only other kindergartner who could read. When my parents forbade me to sleep over at Mark's house, I thought it was because he was Jewish. Years later, embarrassed by what had become of fifties mores, they confessed their bias against little girls spending the night with little boys. Still, I wasn't sure. Jews were more different from Episcopalians than boys were from girls. Already I sensed that such contact was, according to the people in charge, faintly obscene.)

After the Industrial Revolution, the haute bourgeoisie entered the game. With a sponsor linked to the court or the peerage, a wealthy entrepreneur could wangle an invitation to the social events of the season. Arriving in London in 1868, an *arriviste* diarist named Alice Miles noted that "May Manners Sutton, one of the richest and naughtiest of London Grandes Dames, is our great card here; she is rather jealous of Mother who was guilty of the enormous indiscretion of putting her into the shade at Lords the other day, but I am with her constantly, as she imagines I draw the men and don't take possession of them when they arrive."

Indeed, where daughters had once been the coin traded between fiefdoms, they evolved into the industrialists' passport to social acceptance, with money slowly beginning to trump social status. "Sir Samuel tried to inveigle me into a flirtation," notes Alice, "but as I had previously ascertained he has only £4,000 a year which he has abandoned to his mother for the education of his eleven brothers and sisters, there would be no interested side in any such proceedings." Alice herself was forward looking. "I consider it every girl's duty," she told one of her friends, "to marry £80,000 pounds a year, if a beneficent Providence vouchsafes her the opportunity."

After two seasons, Alice found her man; he was a ruthless businessman and the owner of a New Zealand plantation. Untitled and thirty-three years her senior, he had an immense fortune. Social class still mattered, but here's one fork in the road: Alice's mercantile family had gained it merely by having her come out in London.

"Celebration of the Festival of Ceres at St. Louis, October 8 [1878]—the Veiled Prophet chief with his retinue passing the Court House. From sketches by R. Jump." The Grand Oracle on the float is represented by a large statue with scroll and ring. The all-seeing eye at the front is a common symbol of Freemasonry.

The following year, American Masons founded the Mystic Order of Veiled Prophets of the Enchanted Realm, with the eye and "Morcana" as symbolic images. (St. Louis Mercantile Library at the University of Missouri–St. Louis)

She no longer needed to marry *into* society; she *was* society, maintained by her husband's money.

Still, the specially built ballrooms, the presentations, and the displays were all private. Privacy was possible because England was (is), famously, a country of class distinctions. The *Tatler* could write, in 1919, that "a *very* new—*and* rich—Society has risen up since the war and loud, Best Beloved, *very* loud is the knocking at the gate"—but there was always a gate, and lineage on the other side of it.

Contrast America, where former convicts exiled to Georgia emerged from their chrysalises as plantation owners of unparalleled wealth within a generation or two. The fortunate men who ran steamboats up the Hudson or built textile factories in the valleys of western Massachusetts could suddenly outspend the British nobles they had defeated less than a century earlier. How could the feudal tradition of daughter-bartering inform this America of classlessness, Walt Whitman's "interlink'd, food-yielding lands," whose daughters, within memory, would have been hacking at the wilderness alongside their brothers?

The slaveholding South provided the answer for the whole country: race.

Mrs. Bennett's fear that one of her daughters might marry a merchant marine was nothing compared to the Virginia plantation owner's fear of miscegenation. *His* siring of caramel-colored slave children brought life and money to the plantation. His *daughter's* birthing of a similarly tinted baby would foul the blood of the mansion. Witness a court order of the 1690s:

> As much as Ann Wall of this county a free English woman being convicted of having two mulattoe bastards by a negro begotten and borne of her body contrary to ye law, It is therefore ordered that ye said Ann Wall doe serve Mr. Peter Hobson or his assigns the term of five years from ye date hereof and her said two mulatto bastards to serve ye said Hobson in like manner until they attain each of them unto ye age of thirty years.

After serving her term, a woman convicted of miscegenation who had the poor sense to be seen around the county got a one-way ticket to Barbados. The rare—and hence sensational—reports of white women bearing mixed-race children invariably describe these women as lower-class or "of the lower orders." In one peculiar instance, where a plantation wife did give birth to a remarkably dark infant, the cause was elaborately excused. "Upon investigation it was found that a neighbor had been making a 'run' in his liquor still on the day of conception, the fumes had wafted through the lady's house, and she, alas, had breathed too deeply. In a semistupor she had submitted herself to a slave, thinking, understandably, that he was her husband. Thus the unfortunate result was an accident on her part and wholly forgivable."

Whether only impure white women took up with black men or taking up with a black man rendered a woman impure, drawing class boundaries would enforce the race boundary. A process began from a girl's birth, of educating future plantation wives to think of themselves in terms of bloodline. Ballads and romances from the days of English chivalry abounded in plantation libraries. Court masques evoked Ben Jonson. May Day festivals and medieval-style tournaments furthered the illusion that there was indeed a court somewhere, that the plantations constituted medieval castles in latter guise, and that the daughter of the castle should be the knight's fair lady.

Thus was born the southern belle. She took her cues from the antiquated English court and her lineage from the number of slaves her daddy held. She kept up a frenetic social life, knowing that marriage would eventually mean imprisonment. As Emily Putnam wrote in *The Lady*, "Her husband carried her to his plantation and there she lived in isolation. . . . Instead of being the means of a wider freedom, marriage was an abdication."

These presentations and balls, before the Civil War, were still held privately. They represented the last blast of adolescent liberty and the assurance that the belle would become the slave mistress. Preserving the race in her aristocratic body, she would with equanimity sell her husband's yellow progeny down the river.

But Reconstruction drew the next fork in the road. After the war, southerners fought to preserve their traditions of hierarchy and honor, using the image of the former plantation daughter as a nubile shield. "During the fifty years after the Civil War," according to historian Florence Cook, "genteel southerners worked to solidify white supremacy without having to accept the semi-democratic implication that the classification of all white people as superior to all black people made all white people equal. They presented the ideal of the pure Southern lady as proof that they deserved to be at the top of a hierarchical society." Genteel southerners read Sir Walter Scott. They blessed the knights of the Ku Klux Klan. They crowned the Queens of Love and Beauty who would eventually marry Kings.

And suddenly the debutante ball was about marriage only in its remotest and most negative sense. Suddenly, the presentation was public. Lined up in a hotel ballroom or a reconstructed civic center, in their virginal white dresses with their white roses clutched at their alabaster breasts, my predecessors looked indeed like brides awaiting grooms at a mass wedding. Yet they weren't looking for mates the way the girls had at the Regency's private balls. They were announcing—publicly announcing—their inaccessibility.

"Southern white women have preserved the integrity of their race," said Mississippi senator Theodore Bilbo in 1938, "and there is no one who can today point the finger of suspicion in any manner at the blood which flows in the veins of white sons and daughters of the South."

Look all you want, says the public ball, but don't you touch. If they are indeed unspotted from the world, it is the world that must see their spotlessness. Like the tree falling in the wood, the fertile purity they will bring exists only insofar as it is witnessed.

❇   ❇   ❇

This was the element in which I swam in 1972—a year when, let us not forget, the recognition of female race results in the Boston Marathon was a controversial matter. Go back just one year, and 50 percent of American men believed that police "should shoot ghetto rioters." Go back seven years, to my cousin Mimi's presentation, and St. Louis's Veiled Prophet Ball was broadcast regularly on television. My brother and I watched it. A Jewish housewife named Jane Sauer—who, in December 1972, would drive to Kiel Auditorium in disguise and gain entry to the ball with an ill-got ticket—used to watch it. Ntozake Shange, who later wrote *For Colored Girls Who Have Considered Suicide,* watched it on her family's black-and-white set on St. Louis's south side. Presumably there were those in Jefferson City and Springfield and the hill towns of the Ozarks who watched the odd pageantry on their rabbit-eared sets. Milton Berle followed by the Prophet. More public, I suspect, you cannot get.

Our set, too, was black and white—and the year of Mimi's coming out, 1965, I was peeved not to be able to attend the ball in living color. That year, like every year, my father got his tails out of the hanging bag in the attic and slicked back his hair. He would be, he informed us, an usher. Not the Prophet—no, not he. He would not tell us who the Prophet was. His eyes twinkled at the secret.

"They weigh as much as a suitcase," my mother said of his tails.

"Good wool," said my father. "I've had these tails since Yale."

"They make them lighter now," said my mother. "With thinner lapels. Those smell musty," she said, and wrinkled her nose.

I thought my father looked sharp in the tails. He looked rich, like the other dads, and he smiled in his tails like a gentle and lucky man of affairs. With our neighbor, John Lashly, my father left early for Keil Auditorium, kissing me damply on the cheek like a man off on a mission.

My mother lingered. She smelled of Chanel and face powder. She wore a strapless black dress, with pearls around her neck and sling-back heels on her tiny feet. In sixth grade, my brother Dan and I didn't need a babysitter. Mrs. Lashly—heavy around the hips, in cream and rhinestones, long white gloves—honked the horn, and my mother was gone.

We looked for my father on TV, but we never saw him. We watched the set in my parents' room rather than the one in the basement, not because it was better but because it was our parents'. Dan ate a whole bag of Fritos that he'd bought with his own money. Sitting on the black walnut stool at my mother's vanity, I tried on one thing and another. I especially liked the opals, even though she had told me they were bad luck. Our parents' room was done in beige and caramel; I found it ugly. As I sat at the vanity, looking into my mother's huge mirror at the TV behind me, I could see the Maids and Special Maids advance. They appeared very tiny on the set, and of course they were shades of gray, but you could use your imagination.

"Look," said my brother, "that's Ann Day's sister."

"Where?" I said.

"At the curtain, ready to go on. Look how that page is screwing up!"

"Where?"

"*There.* See how she dropped a corner of the train?"

Dan seemed very involved. "This first part's boring," I said.

"So what?" said Dan. He was kneeling smack in front of the set, rocking on his heels.

"It's the same as last year," I said.

But I didn't move; I kept watching, in reverse, in the mirror. Something like fifty times, the trumpets in Kiel Auditorium blew and a man dressed in what I instinctively thought of as *livery* stepped in front of the throne and dais where the Veiled Prophet sat. He unrolled a scroll and read in a deep voice—*a sonorous voice* the newspaper would report the next day:

> *His Mysterious Majesty, the Veiled Prophet!*
> *Welcomes!*
> *To his Court! Of Love and Beauty!*
> *Miss! Carol! Ann! Elsaesser!*

He stretched the "ee" sound in *mysterious* and the "ay" sound in *Veiled*; he rolled the "r" of *Prophet.* It was, as one snippy critic had written, a "home-made archaic language" suggesting a walk "in a field of melting marshmallows." But it held me there, on my mother's little wooden stool. Watching.

As the orchestra started up, a young lady appeared at the end of the auditorium, her white-gloved arm looped into the elbow of a man who could as well have been our dad—same tails, same slicked-back hair and streaks of gray. They advanced; the camera moved in close. Shyly and nervously she turned her head from one side of the auditorium to the other while the audience clapped. The camera homed in on her moist face, mascara'd eyes, lips half-parted in a hesitant smile. For a moment I was afraid it was Mimi. But it wasn't.

"Tina Elsaesser," I said to Dan. "She's pretty ugly."

"She's okay."

"No, she's not. Look at her chin. It's like a man's chin."

He shrugged. He didn't care how they looked. He was interested in something evidently more important. Set free by her escort, Tina Elsaesser bowed to the Veiled Prophet—this was one of those bows I would start practicing in Upper School dance class, all the way to the floor and back up without your knees cracking—and His Majesty acknowledged her with a quick bob of his veiled head.

The trumpets sounded again.

"Here comes Mimi," said Dan.

I swung off the stool and crouched next to him. The chips were gone, but he'd brought up four cans of Tab, with the new pull tops. I ripped one open and tasted the saccharine fizz.

"She *sparkles,*" I said.

Announced with an extra flourish of trumpets and a nimble-stepped parade of little pages in what the announcer was inform-ing us were green bloomers and red tights, Maid Marion Platt Ferriss stepped forward. She was my father's brother's child; she and her older sister, Carol, had been my favorite summer babysitters. Now she stood tall and lovely on the white carpet, a vision caught by the curved screen in my parents' bedroom. Her gown, we were being informed, was pure white poult-de-soie with a high scoop neckline and molded bodice. What glittered in the spotlights were crystals and iridescents in lover's knot designs on the bodice. Her brown curls sat high on the crown of her head and cascaded down her neck. I stroked my own hair, flyaway locks that my mother would not allow me to grow past the nape. Mimi stepped forward, her forehead high and clear. Her lips and chin seemed to me to have a neatness, as if they'd been copied from something more extravagantly beautiful but also messier.

"I like her eyes," I said when I could breathe. "They look like Twiggy's."

Her escort—shorter than she, and balding, recognized by Dan from some father-son event where he had poured on too much barbecue sauce—released my cousin. She bowed and sat. I sipped my Tab. That was all there was to it. The trumpets sounded, the next one came out. Over and over, more than four dozen of them.

The camera did not linger over the Prophet. He was sitting on his throne like the pope, white robes to his ankles, clutching a gold scepter. On his head floated a hat, similar to the dunce-cap head-gear worn by Klansmen in the pictures that Busybee Striker showed us in seventh grade, but with a curtain of white linen covering his face. I could see his ears, with their complicated whorls, in between his hat and veil. They were terribly little. I found my mother's Q-tips in her second drawer. I scooped orange wax out of my ears.

"Here come the Special Maids," said Dan.

"Mimi should have been a Special Maid," I said.

"Wasn't Carol a Special Maid?"

I shook my head. I couldn't remember. Carol had begun to go wild, according to adults. But now the first Special Maid emerged, and I didn't know her. "Goessling," said Dan.

"I've heard the name."

"They go to Harbor Beach."

I leaned into the set. Harbor Beach was the summer place where our family went, on the Michigan thumb. We had relatives there, fourth cousins twice removed. The rich St. Louisans went to Point aux Barques, at the thumb tip. "Sure," I said, still doubtful. "I saw her with Mimi, once."

The Goessling girl didn't sparkle the way Mimi had. Her gown was fuller and longer (". . . empire silhouette," the announcer was saying, "with a cotillion neckline"), and a page brought up her train. Clutching her bouquet of reportedly yellow roses, she turned left and bowed—to the ground, hold to the count of five, up—and the crowd went wild. She then bowed to the other side, facing the cameras. The band switched from Debussy to Chopin. She approached the dais alone, with her head held high, majestic as a sacrifice. I sipped my Tab, tears in my eyes. With the help of another page she made it up the steps, to the very feet of the Prophet, where she crumpled her knees again and dipped her head like a swan. The Prophet stood up, then bent to place the tiara on her head.

The violins swelled. As she took her seat—two steps down and to the left, in front of the bevy of Maids—the pages arranged her train, curling it like a fat comma on the white carpet.

"Mimi's still the prettiest," I said, three Special Maids later.

"The last one was a cow," said Dan.

"Ssh," I said.

On the TV, a hush had settled over the auditorium. The announcer's nasal voice came on the air. "Once again, ladies and gentlemen, the Special Maids are Lauren Noel Goessling, blah, blah, and blah. They have received their crowns from His Mysterious Majesty. The assembled crowd is now waiting eagerly for the appearance of the Prophet's chosen Queen. The cream silk brocade gown for Miss Blah was created by Miss Perkins' Formalwear in Clayton. Miss Blah's gown with its distinctive watteau back comes from Famous-Barr. Miss Blah's Greek-style—oh, wait, ladies and gentlemen, here comes the announcement from the herald."

"Is he the same guy who does football reporting?" I asked Dan.

"Naw. That's a different guy."

"He sounds the same."

"That's just because he's on TV. The other guy has that kind of smeary voice. Like, you know, he says, 'The Shaint Louish Hawksh.'"

The pages were doing a little dance. They were all girls, but they were dressed as boys, and my mother had said they came from a dance school downtown. A couple of years earlier I had wanted to be a page, but she had laughed at the idea. At first I took offense— I thought I was a pretty good dancer; I'd studied four years of ballet. Now, squatting on my parents' beige carpet, I was beginning to understand: the Queen had never been a page, the pages wouldn't grow up to be Queens.

"Betsy Payne," I whispered. Betsy Payne would be Queen. They hadn't called her name yet, but she was my favorite senior at Mary Institute two years past. I used to watch her in the hallways, her lemon hair curling softly around her ears, her delicately sculpted jaw, her forehead with its widow's peak, her sharp eyelashes, her smile like summer. In the yearbook next to each senior's photo (cashmere shell, pearls) were listed her activities, reminding me of the badges I'd sewn onto my Girl Scout sash: the more activities listed, the better the senior. All Mimi had listed were the yearbook and Playworkers. Among Betsy Payne's listed accomplishments were Athletic Association (president); varsity letters in hockey, basketball, and volleyball (captain); copy editor of the yearbook; Summer in France; and Playworkers. I had dared to ask her to sign my yearbook. "Best of luck," she had written in loopy cursive, "during your ensuing years at M.I."

It had to be Betsy Payne.

The herald pulled out his scroll and began again, stretching vowels and rolling *R*s. The orchestra was silent. Finally, after more rolling than seemed strictly necessary, he hit on the name— Rebecca Wells Jones—and the floodlights swung to the doorway at the end of the white carpet.

"You know her?" my brother asked.

Betsy Payne! I was thinking. What happened to Betsy Payne? Suddenly, I was ashamed, not having known. Betsy Payne wasn't a Maid at all. She wasn't at the ball. She hadn't been invited. I swallowed. Kneeling like a cat before the TV set, I said, "They get so gussied up."

"Well, *she* is ugly."

"No, she's not." The Queen was smiling like Miss America, turning her head from side to side. It wasn't her fault that she wasn't Betsy. She had on that frosted lipstick I wanted—I could imagine a teeny hint of pink. Her gown scooped in back, and you could tell she had a good tan. The orchestra moved on to Schubert. The pages—two of them for the Queen, holding her train like a great wave behind her—stepped stiff-legged, eyes straight ahead. She made the bow. All the way to the floor this time, her left knee under that dress surely gracing the carpet.

"She's got orchids," I said.

"How can you tell?" said Dan. He peeled open another Tab.

"They're floppier than roses. You can tell."

The bouquet shook as she straightened. Her nose and teeth were a little big, I thought to myself, but not big enough to dismiss her. She went into the second bow, and I rose. I bowed, queenlike, on the carpet. "Look at this," I said to Dan. I set down the pull tops I'd been playing with, their flat rings and curled aluminum

The 1965 Queen, Rebecca Wells Jones, center, with her Special Maids, Veiled Prophet Parade, 1965. Debutantes ceased to appear in the parade when protests mounted in the late 1960s. (St. Louis Mercantile Library at the University of Missouri–St. Louis)

tongues. Rocking my fanny back on my left heel, I curved my neck forward. Slowly, in time to the music, I rose. I didn't shake one bit. "Pretty good, huh?"

"You won't be Queen."

"Aunt Ann was Queen."

"You won't be. Dad's not Grampop. Grampop was head of the Investment Bankers Association. Dad's just a judge."

"A judge is something."

"A judge isn't much."

"At least I can do the bow. Hopie can't do the bow. I watched her in Dance the other day. She wouldn't even try."

"Well, it's over."

The Queen had folded herself onto the carpet before the Prophet. He had put a crown on her head—same as the tiaras, but heavier, with two layers of rhinestones. Beaming, she was taking her place on the smaller throne, to his right and slightly below him. As Dan snapped off the set, the cameras were enlarging a view of her face, the tears of happiness coursing from her eyes. It was just like *Queen for a Day*. I worried about her mascara. Maybe she had the waterproof kind.

❅   ❅   ❅

Mimi's year would be the last year of the television broadcast, though we didn't know it at the time. It was also the first year of protests, by a then-fringe group, against its very existence. But the announcer had said nothing about the protests, nothing about the discomfort in the streets. My brother left the fading blue light of the TV to go work in his room on an intricate model aircraft carrier. I brushed my teeth by the night-light in the bathroom and then lingered by the front window.

It was October then; the ball, in those days, took place the night before the parade, that ultimate public display of power, where Becky Jones and the Goessling girl would ride on a float and wave at the crowd like slow-motion windshield wipers. Outside, a fine drizzle brushed the house. Leaves trembled on the young linden trees, planted last spring in honor of our street's name. Oaks on Oak Circle, I thought; cherry trees on Cherry Lane. The other

streets in our part of town were named after war heroes and former
city officials. The grass of our lawn glistened with rain. Tomorrow
would clear, my father had promised before he went out; in eighty-
seven years, the Prophet had failed only twice to provide fine
October parade weather for his beloved city.

Although I couldn't see past the rise of the next street over, the
sky was pale in that direction, from the lights of Pershing Boulevard leading downtown. My parents were going on to the dance at
the Chase Park Plaza. In three or four hours they would be driving
back along the winding boulevard that bisected Forest Park—
together by then, in our car, their elegant clothes persuading them
toward civility with one another. The wind picked up, blowing
scattered yellow leaves.

Within two or three years, Forest Park would become a place
white people didn't walk at night. Later, when I finally got my
driver's license, I would say I was going to my friend Lindy Bowe's
house and would drive her down to Forest Park, where she would
drop a hit of acid and go off with a trio of pimply, long-haired,
laughing boys. Waiting by the Jewel Box till she returned, I would
watch a pair of stoned black people make out on the hill, their
Afros like fat black flowers.

But for now I slipped into a cotton gown and watched the trees
bend and rustle. Opening the window of my bedroom, over the
front porch where I sometimes sneaked out to the roof on summer
nights, I inhaled the fall air, dry even in drizzle. The lightning bugs
had vanished. Only a couple of houses on our block had porch
lights on, waiting for returning adults. The street sloped black and
silent. Across the way, under the lamp, I saw that my brother's friend
Ben had left his bike out to rust. Tomorrow he would be going to
the parade—they all would—but already I didn't care about it, a
bunch of slow-moving floats, marching bands, and candy tossed to
the crowds. The breeze blew soft on my face. October was always
a relief, the dense humidity of September lifted like a blanket.
Lifting my arms by the open window, I mourned Betsy Payne,
who should have been Queen. I wondered if she knew what she
had been robbed of; if jealousy touched her.

If I could have cast my eye farther to the southeast, past the park and Kingshighway where they were holding the Queen's Supper, not so far as Kiel Auditorium but still in the shadow of Highway 40, I'd have made out the twin towers of Pruitt Igoe. If I could have put my ear to the damp ground, I would have heard the rumblings. They were coming to shake the glass of my windows, to toss my King Arthur books from their shelves; they would pop the rhinestones from the tiara of my favorite Special Maid. And then they would go for His Mysterious Majesty, so lonesome on his makeshift throne, forced every year to find and break in a new Queen. They were coming to shake him. They were coming to shake the veil from his face.

Ten

The Other Side

Learn to identify the enemy.

— PERCY GREEN, 1965

During my senior year at Mary Institute, I took a new course called "Urban Studies," offered by a new teacher, Harvey Sperling, a crossover from my brother's school two hockey fields away. Two advantages to taking this class were being able to call the teacher by his first name and locating a research subject in the local community. For my project, I chose the moribund federal housing project, Pruitt-Igoe.

At the time, the only fact I had on Pruitt-Igoe was that a group of black families, driven by the impending doom of the towers, had appealed to the city for alternate housing and been granted a row of abandoned apartment buildings on Clara Street, close to where my grandparents lived. Clara Street was where we would go, often, after church, for Sunday dinners with my pale and elegant grandparents. We reached their pale and elegant apartment, with its original wallpaper, by the original self-operating Otis elevator from the four-story building's narrow lobby.

My grandparents, naturally, moved out as soon as the petition was approved, but my mother followed the progress of the group and was impressed. "They're fixing the elevators," she said over the evening paper. "They've got flowerpots in the windows. They have a sense of community, these people. It's unusual."

Pruitt had originally stood for white; *Igoe* for black. As the only major U.S. metropolis to have declined in population in the 1930s,

St. Louis after the Second World War seemed due for an overhaul. Civic Progress, a group formed by the mayor and a Boatmen's Bank executive named Tom K. Smith, among others, helped to mold the land-use policy that "revitalized" the downtown area and created Pruitt-Igoe.

The idea was to build sets of towers side by side, separate and not only equal but also proximate. The project had begun in 1956, the same year *The Coming of the Veiled Prophet* was published. The first large-scale federally funded housing project to materialize after the war, it was designed by Minoru Yamasaki, who had designed the main terminal at Lambert Field. Yamasaki was a disciple of Le Corbusier, whose postmodern style was beginning to dictate the American skyline; Yamasaki's own greatest fame would later come as the architect of the doomed World Trade Center towers in Manhattan. In fact, Pruitt-Igoe's original thirty-three eleven-story structures were hailed as a "Manhattan-style renovation" for St. Louis, a new city-within-a-city, featuring open galleries and common spaces. During construction, the Supreme Court decisions on segregation dictated that the complex's residents would not be separated according to the color of their skin.

But by the time the project was completed, when I was perhaps ten, inflated construction bids had forced a move toward more buildings, smaller units, and thinner walls. Skip-stop elevators stopped on every other floor, leaving stairwell corners for drug dealing, rape, murder, and anything else that needed a dark trap. Running short of funds, the engineers installed cheap plumbing that sprang leaks and wiring that shorted out. The playgrounds so generously installed (for the children these people insisted on having) were made of asphalt and steel, and they were quickly overtaken by weeds and violence. The whites never moved in; the blacks moved out as soon as they could afford an uninfested apartment elsewhere. By the time I wrote my report, the forty-four towers of Pruitt-Igoe had a 40 percent occupancy rate and the highest crime rate in the city.

"There was no way for us to know," Mr. Kassabaum told me. We sat in the spring sunshine on his back patio. Mr. Kassabaum was a very handsome, sandy-haired man, serious and friendly. His daughter Ann went to John Burroughs School, Mary Institute's rival. In 1965, his firm, Hellmuth, Obata and Kassabaum, closely associated with Yamasaki, had received the contract and the burden of redeveloping and rescuing Pruitt-Igoe. The firm had just that year, 1970, conceded defeat.

I never thought, Yamasaki himself had said of the project's residents, *people were that destructive.*

"Why do you think they were so destructive?" I asked Mr. Kassabaum.

He spread his innocent hands wide. "We built those towers in every expectation of a certain kind of human response," he said. "That response was not forthcoming. Plus, you had the federal government involved. That means waste and excess and cost over-runs. Corners were cut. I've never denied that. The question is, whose corners, and to what end?"

Corners cut, I wrote. It reminded me of the way my grandmother said her Negro maid talked when she was missing a piece of crockery. "That dish got broke, ma'am," the maid would say. Could we imagine? The dish flew itself off the table and got itself broke.

Corners were cut. Harvey circled the sentence in my paper. *Watch passive,* he wrote.

⌗ ⌗ ⌗

Before the blacks moved in on Clara Street and my grandparents moved out, our Sundays there had included a heavy dinner, cooked and served by the maid in whose care the dishes got broke. We used to listen to my stepgrandmother, Grace, play Chopin. Then we were excused to go to Grace's "boudoir," where we would jump on her bed and watch color TV while the adults conversed in the living room.

One winter Sunday, driving down to Clara Street with the windows rolled up, my father stopped the car at a red light on Euclid Avenue. I was in the passenger seat—my mother often declined these invitations—and suddenly my father barked at me, "Lock the door!"

As I turned, frightened, to press down the black button, my eyes met those of a man on the other side of the glass. It was a Negro, crossing the street with the light. He saw me. He watched me press down fast on the lock.

⚌   ⚌   ⚌

Now that guy from the street was out there, outside Kiel Auditorium. They all were—all those people who'd lost their hived homes when Pruitt-Igoe was dynamited earlier that year, at a cost of $300 million, leaving a twenty-acre crater in South St. Louis. They were out in the cold streets, and I had not given them my extra invitations or offered to join them. Inside, warm and safe, was my father. Arriving soon after were his new wife, Nancy; my beautifully coiffed stepgrandmother, Grace; my brother and sister and mother and, unbelievably, Michael Edson. And me.

It was very warm in the basement of the auditorium. Dry and cavernous. Bare bulbs graced the ceilings; the walls were high-gloss yellow. Girls moved in and out of various dressing rooms, attended by uniformed black women whom I mistook for their personal maids. "Famous-Barr sent her," one girl corrected me, glancing at a woman on her knees, tacking up a hem. "You get the service when you buy the dress."

I was jealous. I wanted someone kind and quiet like that tending to my hem. Not that there was anything wrong with my hem, except that it was fuller than the other girls' hems. My bodice was tighter than theirs and my sleeves longer. They all had the gloves, the long white gloves like the pair my mother had saved for me, that buttoned up the forearm.

Well, never mind, never mind. I ducked into a stall in the ladies' room and popped a brownie into my mouth. I could really taste the herb, this time, stronger than the cocoa. I liked the taste, bitter and clean. I picked a bit out of my teeth, then swished and swallowed at the water fountain.

A matron was calling us to attention, ready to give us instructions. "What a joke this whole thing is," I said to the girl on my left. Her name was Muffy Lammert, or had been. People had told me she now wanted to go by her real name, Bartow. Bartow Simeral Hawes Lammert. But in my mind Muffy Lammert was a wiseacre, a plump rich popular girl who didn't hold anything sacred. Now she had lost weight. She wore a peach chiffon gown trimmed in pearls with straps that showed off her shoulders. She was shorter than I remembered, petite even.

"What whole thing?" she said.

"This whole deb thing," I said. Was no one alive any more? "It's just so funny," I said, and gave out a stoned giggle. "All those Fortnightly dance classes and we were all miserable, and we thought they were *over* with. When really they were just *training*. *Look* at us," I said. I swept a purple arm to indicate the low-ceilinged, mustardy room. "Pigs to the slaughter," I said.

"I'm pretty excited, actually," said Bartow. She smiled a tight little smile.

"You can't be," I said.

"Sure," Bartow said. Then after a beat, "Hopie will be Queen."

"Duh," I said.

She moved away, wounded. An unwelcome tear sprang to my eye. I needed to get higher. I needed to get high enough to float over Kiel Auditorium, to look down and see myself, purple in a sea of pastels, a bright unimportant dot.

⁂   ⁂   ⁂

I have not flown that high, not yet. I am only high enough above the past to pick out other characters in this lavish minidrama. Jane Sauer, Margaret Phillips, Gena Scott, and Percy Green. These are the actors I track down, a quarter century after the fact. That night in 1972, they were outside Kiel Auditorium, in the swirling snow, waiting for their chance. Farther offstage lingered the extras— Laura Rand Orthwein, Veiled Prophet Queen of 1959, now known as Laura X; Mary Ann Fitzgerald, who would later loan me her scrapbook of the ACTION years; and Mattie Johnson, who knelt on the floor that evening, tacking up a hem.

Why do we seek out the past when we do? It takes a tragedy for some, like my New England friend Adele, whose son took his own life at the age of thirty-one and who now analyzes her young marriage and, further back, her relationship with her father. Others, like my mother, seek to justify their lives before they are summed up by death and so ask questions to which they want, not answers, but a soothing reminder of the exigencies of fate. Still others, on the brink of unexpected change, go rooting among the shards of the past, seeking patterns.

"When did you start thinking about this?" Tom Spencer asked me in Kirksville, and I gave him a clever answer. Back in the pool house, I ask myself the same question, and I realize that I started remembering the Veiled Prophet story when I was on the witness stand, fifteen years ago. I had been subpoenaed in Manhattan to testify against my former landlord, who had at one point taken everything I owned in an attempt to force me to abandon my wreck of an apartment. The landlord's attorney, a butterball of a man who reminded me of Dom DeLuise, approached the stand with his index finger against his chin. "Now, Miss Ferriss," he said, "you not only hold a day job but you also write fiction. Isn't that right?"

The assistant district attorney had instructed me to confirm anything that was factually true. "That's right," I said.

"You make up stories. Isn't that right?"

"That is right."

"Some of these *stories* are so good, they've been *published*. Isn't that right!"

"That," I said, mortified, "is right."

I was getting a wee bit tired of the world's associating stories with make-believe. I was also witnessing the birth of "New Traditionalism" ads, for pottery and magazines, which featured a successful woman choosing to stay home among her plants and furniture and well-groomed sons. Reports in the mid-1980s of the backlash against feminism and affirmative action bothered me at a level beyond my clearly articulated political stance. I had a story to tell the New Traditionalists, a story I had not made up. If I was going to be on the stand, I wanted to bear witness to the truth in this story. It began with a small anecdote, about a girl who receives a letter.

"Anecdotes don't make good stories," according to the Canadian writer Alice Munro. "The story that finally comes out is not what people thought their anecdotes were about."

Back in St. Louis, digging up the past, I am still asking what the story—of the girl, and of the letter—is about. I pick up the phone in the pool house, my luxurious enclave. I call the next person on my list: Jane Sauer.

⁂   ⁂   ⁂

Jane is one of three villains in the newspaper accounts of the 1972 Veiled Prophet Ball; the other two are Percy Green and Gena Scott, the chief perpetrator. Thus far on my quest, I've not been able to locate Gena Scott, but Jane is listed under her husband's name and responds quickly. She would be happy to talk to me.

I head down Highway 40 to Compton Avenue in the warehouse district, a row of boarded-up buildings where thin black men shuffle warily along the sidewalk. At a reinforced steel door, I ring the bell for Jane's studio. Waiting for her to answer, I try to picture this woman I have never met. During the days when I was attending my father's wedding and waiting for Michael Edson's plane to descend at Lambert Field, Jane Sauer was attending ACTION meetings to plan the 1972 protest of the Veiled Prophet Ball. ACTION's plans were as earnest as they were vague. Gena and Jane were white, well-dressed, soft-spoken women. Using donated tickets, they could get past the door of Kiel Auditorium where Percy Green and the rest of his entourage would be turned away. After that, I cannot think what plans they had, how it all came about.

The keen-eyed woman who opens the door is now a slim but sturdy grandmother, with photos of her daughter's children framed along the wall. Her studio extends back from the entrance into a light-filled space where she makes sinuous sculptures from painted styrofoam molds overlaid with tightly woven, painted linen cord. "There's a lot of mess right now," she explains as we take a tour of the studio. "I have a show in New York coming up and a bunch of new pieces to get ready."

Under the skylights, bright abstract shapes litter long tables. The shapes are inspired, she tells me, by the variety of animals she found in Australia, a few years ago. "You know, those animals that look as if they're made out of leftovers? With a giraffe's neck and a pig's nose. I wanted to create that feeling in these pieces."

Nonhuman though these pieces are, they have a hip-heavy quality, like three-dimensional paisleys. They seem to be asking questions. Some of their tails curl into one another, as if they are posing for an affectionate photograph. Some forms are still at an early stage, the cloth not yet woven on, and they fool the onlooker. They look like burnished iron, sleek and heavy. I go to pick one up expecting to strain, and the shape almost flies out of my hand.

Jane lives not far from here, in the Central West End of St. Louis. "But back then, I was with my first husband in Creve Coeur," she explains. We're sitting now; Jane has made tea. Taking time out from finishing touches, she seems relieved to sink into the small couch in the shank of the studio and let her hands rest. "It was the suburbs, the other side of Ladue," she says. "All white, all the same. I hated it."

Her husband liked to keep kosher; Jane didn't care about it one way or the other. On Passover and other holy days, to please him, she would go down to the basement and fetch the two sets of dishes. It was while carrying these dishes, in 1968, that Jane heard the call to political action. As she came up the stairs, her daughters were watching TV in the living room. It was one of those somber announcements that begins, "We interrupt this program." A man named James Earl Ray, the newscaster was saying, had shot and killed the Reverend Dr. Martin Luther King.

"I just stood there with the dishes in my hands," Jane says, "and I thought, 'What am I doing? What am I doing?'"

I suck in my breath. I refrain from sharing the cartoon I found while rummaging through old copies of the conservative *St. Louis Globe-Democrat* newspaper. The drawing, dated March 31, 1968—four days before the King assassination—is of a thuggish-looking King looking vacantly ahead with a tricked-up halo behind his head and a magnum pistol in his hand, firing indiscriminate bullets labeled "looting," "trouble," "violence." Accompanying the cartoon is a long editorial on "The Real Martin Luther King." It's possible that it was written by Pat Robertson, who cut his journalistic teeth on the editorial page of the *Globe*. The piece accuses King of "inflammatory speeches," of causing "riotous outbreaks."

"He is proving," reads the editorial, "to be one of the most menacing men in America today."

I don't mention this bit of trivia to Jane Sauer. I am ashamed of my family's loyal subscription to the *Globe-Democrat,* of my parents' belief in its opinions, of its loyal endorsement, every four years, of Franklin Ferriss for circuit judge.

"Not long after King's death," Jane is saying, "I saw a notice on a billboard, something about an ACTION meeting."

She had heard there was such a group; she'd seen some of the leaders' faces in the papers. Not knowing if a white Jewish housewife would be welcome, she drove east from homogeneous Creve Coeur to a downtown address. "The meeting was in a black neighborhood, and I remember all these cars passing me, and I thought they were all going to the meeting. I had this really inflated idea of the size of this group that was making itself heard. I'd see a car go by with black people in it and park, and I'd think, 'They must be going to the meeting.' I was so surprised to get there and find out the true size. There was really just a handful of people, then."

Percy Green led the meeting. He was young and imposing. He wore a dark beret and a black T-shirt with the ACTION logo emblazoned across the front. It had been four years at that point, Jane tells me, since he had come to public attention with his demonstration at the Gateway Arch. Climbing the steel frame with plastic suction cups, he had launched the most flamboyant protest against job discrimination the city had ever seen, and in a single day the whites-only policy for Arch construction workers was dropped. White people, Jane knew, were afraid of Percy Green.

"In fact, though, within the organization, he was very pure, very straight-laced," Jane says. She speaks with a slightly nasal accent that mixes New York heritage with midwestern twang. "Percy warned us about getting caught with marijuana. He monitored members' romantic lives—he didn't want us getting caught in some sexual scandal. He always talked about how the opposition would just love to get us in trouble that way. And he knew how to use white female members. He had that part all figured out, how to get our faces out there."

When Percy targeted the Veiled Prophet, Jane latched on. She had grown up watching the parade. Every year she would gather with her family at the front of the silent crowd on Market Street to view the elaborate floats. Tentatively, she would wave back at the blond Queen, in the long white gloves, who'd been crowned the

Percy Green climbing the Gateway Arch, June 1964. Behind him is his fellow demonstrator, Richard Daly. The two men sat on a girder 125 feet above the ground for four hours to protest discrimination in hiring for the Arch project. (St. Louis Mercantile Library at the University of Missouri–St. Louis)

Percy Green after his descent from the Arch. Following civil disobedience guidelines, he went limp as he was arrested. (St. Louis Mercantile Library at the University of Missouri–St. Louis)

night before. "'Someday,' I said to my mother, 'I'm going to be that Queen. I'm going to wear that headache band and that ostrich feather.' I knew how you could turn that jewel holding the feather into a brooch. I dreamed about pinning that brooch to my wedding dress, which is what I'd heard all the Queens did. You know what my mother said? She said, 'It's not for girls like you. They don't pick Jewish girls.'"

Her partner on that cold night in 1972, Jane confirms, was Gena Scott—the same Gena Scott who had been arrested ten months earlier with Margaret Phillips for entering the F-15 bomber room at McDonnell Douglas.

"I've been trying to find Gena Scott," I say. "That trial was held in my father's courtroom."

Jane lifts an eyebrow. "You do have an interesting history, don't you?"

"Do you know where she is? Do you know what she's doing?"

"She's a real estate agent these days." Jane picks at a thread in her slacks. "I think she does some art as well. But we're not in touch. She was always in it for different reasons than I was."

"What were your reasons?" I ask.

"It was a community," she says quickly. "We watched each other's kids when someone had to go to a demonstration. We had barbecues together. We were a lot of different types of people living near each other, working together. That was how it worked, for a while."

For a while, I think. As an investigative reporter, I am all thumbs. I want to ask, "And then what?"—but the question seems prurient, gossipy, picking over the bones of a dead movement to find its internal malfunctions. So much has been written to expose the revolutionary groups of that time, to pronounce their members— guess what?—human. Fallible.

"ACTION was a great thing, I think," I say, instead. "It accomplished much of its purpose."

"It did, didn't it?" Jane's chin lifts. "And it wasn't all grim, you know. There were some very funny people."

We say our good-byes. In the garage at the back of the studio, we pass by Jane's SUV, sized to hold her artwork. One of the studio's attractions, she points out, has been its locked private garage space. That this precaution is entirely reasonable does not prevent some appreciation of its irony from crossing my face. "And what about you?" Jane asks on my way out the door.

"What about me?" I say.

"Did you marry one of your own?" she asks.

I know what the question means. And in the sense with which it is asked, the answer is no. But it is not my husband's social status that crosses my mind; it is my own. "I don't know," I say. "I'm still trying to find that out."

Eleven

On the Carpet

*Now it was my turn. There was a
breathless pause, no sound could you
hear except the beating of my heart.*

— GRACE DODD, Special Maid, 1894

I've been in St. Louis almost a week when I finally track down Gena Scott. She is, as Jane Sauer suggested, a real estate agent now, and I locate her at an agency that specializes in the revived Central West End. At first, we just speak on the phone. I perch on a bar stool in the pool house, sipping a concoction from my host's reserves, while I scribble down her answers. Gena Scott's voice on the phone is gravelly, a smoker's alto. She is not originally from St. Louis but arrived here in the sixties from Minnesota by way of Iowa. She still has her northern Midwest twang, with the Scandinavian rounding of the *o*. When Scott moved to St. Louis, civil rights were nowhere on her agenda.

"It wasn't like I didn't know there were race problems," she says. "But it was the sixties. I was protesting the Vietnam War."

"Me too," I say, a little too quickly.

"And feminism? Who had heard of feminism? I followed my husband to St. Louis. He had a job at IBM. I held all kinds of jobs. I painted. At one point I had my own shop, in the Central West End. Then my husband got involved in this group called Action against Apathy. They were backed by local community groups, church groups. A number of Catholic nuns were members. Their focus was mostly education. That's what we thought would solve the race question, education. So they were trying to desegregate the schools and all that."

But they weren't, Gena says, getting anything done. Her husband stuck with the group, but she found another, this time with ACTION in capital letters. "They had their fingers in everything," she says while I scribble. "Protests against the war. Lobbies for better jobs, for better public schools and housing. Protests against the Arch. And then of course the VP Ball. But I don't want to go into that until we've met. I mean, there have been a lot of people over the years asking me questions."

"Tom Spencer?" I say.

"Yes, that guy. And others. But I didn't like that guy. I've wanted to put some distance between myself and the past. Now—I don't know. Maybe we can talk."

We hang up.

I pull out my copies of the June 15, 1972, *St. Louis Post-Dispatch* article on Gena Scott's and Margaret Phillips's convictions for trespassing at McDonnell Douglas. In the accompanying picture, both young women are wearing sleeveless blouses—Margaret's white, Gena's black—in what I remember as the leathery humidity of the St. Louis County Courthouse. Margaret looks smart and stern, Gena like a young Mary Tyler Moore, pretty and awkward. The newspaper reports that they had acted as their own attorneys and had vetted jurors by asking their opinion of the musical *Hair.* The one juror who liked the show was disqualified by the prosecutor.

Their trial had taken place during the last summer I spent in St. Louis. Living for the first and only time in my mother's new ranch house, having rejected my former counseling job at the county parks day camp, I trudged door to suburban door selling Avon creams and perfumes in their kitschy jars. That summer my mother had made me two long sleeveless summer dresses in bright, pretty prints to wear to the debutante parties that dotted the calendar like tornado warnings. I tried them both on and announced that I would wear neither, then drove downtown and bought myself a cheap batik-print version with a halterlike neck.

(Did my mother cry? I am sure she cried. In the warming days of May she had shopped for the crisp cotton and the tricky Butterick patterns. With her quick hands she had run the seams through the ancient black chain-stitch machine she had inherited from her own mother. She had hemmed the dresses by hand, catching the thread in each stitch so the hems would not run. She had held them, finished, before her own trim figure in the full-length mirror of her new house and had pictured her vivacious and popular daughter. In fewer than ten words I dismissed a week's worth of effort. But she did not cry in front of me. She tightened her lips and shrugged. I remember the dresses in every detail, including the elegant keyhole neck of one and the way it draped over my forbidden collarbone. But they were never worn.)

Midway through July of that summer, I took off with three other young women to Captiva Island, Florida, where we lay on the white sand in front of another debutante's family villa. Then I borrowed the girl's car and took it across Alligator Alley to visit my college friend John in Miami. We sat up all night smoking pot, listening to Richie Havens, and plotting the ouster of Richard Nixon.

Gena, meanwhile, according to my photocopied newspaper report, had organized a hunger strike to protest unsanitary conditions at the women's low-security prison. And there, on the same page of the newspaper, is the announcement that the Veiled Prophet Society had come up with its theme for the fall parade, "Happiness Is . . ." The ball had been moved, several years earlier, to December, to accommodate debutantes who'd gotten serious about college. But the parade stayed where it was, in the dry warmth of early October. Instead of the VP Queen, Miss America 1972 would wave from one of the floats, which had helium balloon representations of happiness—an elf, a giant, and a panda bear—floating high overhead.

Perched on my bar stool in the pool house, I think about the meaning of happiness. The happiness of the parade, according to the *St. Louis Post-Dispatch,* turned out to be "nothing startling. A warm puppy. Taking a vacation . . . . Having a hobby—collecting butterflies." The Southwest High School Band had marched through the streets, playing "American Pie." Protesters had stood silent on the sidelines, and the all-black Vashon Band had made it to the parade despite having had the tires on its buses slashed by ACTION protesters that morning. For none of the people in these blue-collar and nonwhite groups was the happiness of collecting butterflies a foreseeable attainment.

I am reminded of the story "The Ones Who Walk Away from Omelas" by the fantasy writer Ursula Le Guin. In this story, Le Guin suggests that happiness as most people define it is predicated on not only the existence but also the awareness—yea, the acceptance—of another's misery.

> The child used to scream for help at night, and cry a good deal, but now it only makes a kind of whining, "eh-haa, eh-haa," and it speaks less and less often. It is so thin there are no calves to its legs; its belly protrudes; it lives on a half-bowl of corn meal and grease a day. It is naked. Its buttocks and thighs are a mass of festered sores, as it sits in its own excrement continually. They all know it is there, all the people of Omelas. . . . They all understand that their happiness, the beauty of their city, the tenderness of their friendships, the health of their children, the wisdom of their scholars, the skill of their makers, even the abundance of their harvest and the kindly weathers of their skies, depend wholly on this child's abominable misery.

Le Guin's ironic happiness seems to suit the joy of the 1972 parade, though I was not there to witness the balloons or the protesters. Happiness still seemed to me to belong in fairy tales— or in the manifesto of the revolution, when the pursuit to which Thomas Jefferson had said we were entitled would finally land its carefree quarry.

Still, the professional photo taken of me at the ball, on the arm of Fred Schlafly as I prepared to step into the auditorium, shows a young woman beaming like a lightbulb. Her breasts push, pert and round as softballs, against the clinging fabric of her gown. Her expression spells the vapid bliss of marijuana. All her effort seems to go into holding her eyelids open wide, weighted as they are with mascara, and her mouth has gone a little crooked as she smiles for the photo. Fred Schlafly wears his VP ribbon and medallion. His face is mostly chin. He is having, no doubt about it, the time of his life.

Later, my mother would tell me the matron in the box behind her leaned toward a companion and whispered, at sight of my candy-cane dress, "They'll wear *anything* these days."

Entering the arena, I did not hear the comment. I heard only the adenoidal swell of the trumpets and the muffled clapping of thousands of gloved hands. The fourth brownie had transported me to the exact spot where I stood, two hundred feet of red carpet away from His Mysterious Majesty, who was sitting humble as the pope on his dais. I walked as my mother had taught me, as if a string suspended me through the center of my head. My dyed heels brought me to the bottom of the stairs. I let go of Mr. Schlafly's arm and I bowed. For the last time I regretted my status as mere Maid, which precluded me from bowing all the way to the floor. I could have done it without shaking, without my knees cracking. Had I held orchids, they would not have trembled. But I placed my right leg behind my left and bent my knees, in willing obeisance, and the Prophet blessed me with his secular scepter, and my left leg propelled me back up. Mr. Schlafly took my arm again. We were going to be married; his chin alone could support me for the rest of my life. We would have a dozen children and they would frolic in our garden, and I would wear frocks and trim the roses. The world ahead was full of grace, unspotted.

Mr. Schlafly guided me to my seat, an armless Queen Anne chair set among the others. "Thank you," he whispered in my ear.

"Thank *you,*" I said.

Oh, baby. I may not have been happy, but I was high. High would do, for now.

⁂ ⁂ ⁂

"Meanwhile," says Gena Scott, drinking a gin and tonic across from me at Montego's on Laclede Place, "Jane and I got all dressed up. We were afraid someone would *recognize* us. Jane put on make-up for the first time since high school. I got my dress at Saks on Maryland. It was sort of Oriental in cut and design—a jersey fabric, kind of clingy, with long sleeves."

"Mine, too," I said. "It was the wrong dress."

"It was different in style. The skirt had a little swing at the ankle.

But a Nehru collar. Very covered up. And we wore heels."

Gena's voice is more attractive in person than it is on the phone. In person, the gravelly tone of her voice is warmer, even melodic. Everyone who knew her in the seventies has remarked on her beauty then, and it's still there, albeit sanded down by time—the high cheekbones and flat, olive-skinned cheeks, full mouth, and Roman nose. She gives her hair a slight toss each time a new idea comes to her. At the time she's speaking of, December 1972, she had just split from her husband, who didn't much like his wife's turn toward the radical. She had lost her job at Southwestern Bell when she testified before the Missouri Public Service Commission about rate inequities in Missouri. She had argued with her husband over their white-bread, suburban life.

"We had sold our place in Des Moines for a nice profit in '69," she says. "And what had attracted me right off in St. Louis was the Central West End. Those terrific old buildings, and the life that was around there. But the agents were reluctant to show us houses there. They told us horror stories—you know, higher taxes and utilities, dangerous streets, declining property values. They kept taking us out to the county. And then banks were redlining. They wanted 50 percent down for a purchase in the Central West End. Finally my husband went along with the real estate agent, and we bought a house in Kirkwood. I only lasted a year there."

Having left her husband, she had begun writing a column for the *St. Louis American* with the byline "ACTION Education Chrm." After the McDonnell trial, she had won reforms at the women's prison; she had returned to graduate school; she had taken part in Percy Green's annual protests outside Kiel Auditorium. Then, in 1972, she was admitted to the ball.

"At first Jane and I just milled around," she says. "We were having fun. We were undercover, in disguise. I mean, we were white, we were dressed up, we had the invitations. All the black people with invitations had been turned away and were outside protesting."

"Who got you the invitations?" I ask.

"Percy. He'd gotten them from some debutantes."

"But what debs? Do you have names?"

Gena shakes her head. "They were good seats. Third balcony, though—you could only be admitted to the balcony listed on your ticket. We sat there awhile, then we climbed higher, where we could look down on the scene. But then you know what? It got boring. I mean, it was the same thing. Over and over. The trumpets and the marching and the reading out of the names. First the matrons, and each one walks the perimeter, and then the girls each walk the plank before bowing to the Prophet. I saw you people sitting up there on the stage, sitting so quiet. I don't know how you could stand it, going on for hours. Boring."

"I was stoned," I say.

"Everyone looked stoned. People were just looking for something to happen."

"And then," I said, "you happened."

Gena Scott smiles at me, over the rim of her glass. For half a moment, I am eighteen again, and she is twenty-four, and we are both ready for things to happen.

Twelve

The Magic Land of Khorassan

*I, the Black Veiled Prophet, demand to enter
this KKK rally. My mission is to radiate
love, joy, and above all, human justice.*

— MAJOR WILLIAM BROWN, ACTION Guerrilla Force, 1969

While driving around St. Louis, I listen to a local public radio station. Discussions about the state of the city fill the airwaves. How exactly does St. Louis lag behind other cities? Why? What can well-meaning citizens do to "get people involved"? A group of young people called Metropolis St. Louis welcomes new members and suggestions for urban renewal. Listeners call in. One man says that he prefers Atlanta; another says Minneapolis. A third person calls in to boast of his children, who went to the four corners of the globe and came back to St. Louis to live because it had everything they wanted. The hosts, guests, and callers are, as far as I can tell, all white people.

At Margaret Phillips's suggestion I drive out to meet with Mary Ann Fitzgerald. Mary Ann had nothing in particular to do with the Veiled Prophet protest but remains a devoted chronicler of ACTION and its times. The neatly kept nineteenth-century frame house where she and her husband live and have raised their kids slants with the pitch of the land toward the street. They live in Ferguson, a predominantly white blue-collar community that borders Kinloch, the poorest black community in St. Louis County.

"When I was still Catholic," Mary Ann says over Diet Coke in her big square living room, "we started going to church in Kinloch because they had a kindergarten and Ferguson didn't have a kindergarten. And my policy was to get the children out to school as quick as you could." She makes a shooing motion and laughs. "But the neighbors were mad. Some of the people in the parish here wouldn't talk to us after we started going to Kinloch. I said to my kids, 'Those people are racists.' Then after I got involved with ACTION we'd have a huge party here every year. Oh, there would be a hundred and fifty people in this house! And food for everyone, we had a great time. And I told my children they could invite all the friends they wanted to the party, only no racists."

Mary Ann is one of those women whose age is hard to tell—a slight figure, short dyed brown hair, and a small efficient face with no wrinkles. Her thin-rim glasses sport a line of turquoise on the top, and the right frame is chipped. She has never, I suspect, felt sorry for herself.

She tells me that she had given birth to eight children in the course of nine years when her Catholicism drew her out of her home and into the streets with Percy Green. "I had finally gotten on the Pill by then," she said. "I went to three priests to confess it. And they each said, 'Well, if your doctor has prescribed this medication, then it can't be a sin for you to take it.' I didn't choose easy priests, either. I wanted to be sure my conscience was clear."

A religious member of ACTION, Sister Cecilia of the Maryknoll order, had chained herself to a revolving door at a Famous-Barr department store to call attention to the plight of black families for whom the Christmas buying season was a nightmare of debt. Mary Ann heard the news on the radio at home and "fired off a telegram" to the jailed nun. That evening she handed over her youngest, who was still in diapers, to her husband when he got home late from work and announced that she was going to a demonstration to support Sister Cecilia. "I told him not to wait up," she says.

She grins a little puckishly. After demonstrating for Sister Cecilia's release, Mary Ann signed on with ACTION. She had already met Percy Green through her work. After eight years of doing her duty at home, "ends just weren't meeting." With a high-school education, she'd set out to find what she could by way of work. She read an editorial announcing that the National Opinion Research Center, at the University of Chicago, would be conducting a thousand interviews in black St. Louis neighborhoods, asking residents the question "How does power evolve?" Mary Ann was the only white person hired to be an interviewer, and she found herself inside the homes of the black community for the first time. By the time Sister Cecilia was jailed, Mary Ann's eye was on news stories coming out of the civil rights movement in the South. She was reading James Baldwin and Richard Wright. And the gestures of the young Percy Green had fired her imagination. "That time he climbed the Arch," she says, "I was moved to tears. I thought, 'Well, if he can do that, I ought to do *something*.'"

Mary Ann was soon going to churches on what Percy Green called Black Sundays and interrupting services to read a statement about the churches' dearth of commitment to civil rights. For a good Catholic girl, it was a lesson in confrontation. "This one woman spat at me, full in the face," she says, running her open palm down the length of her petite features. "I think I had the presence of mind to say 'Bless you.' I hope I said it. But I can't be sure."

Burning a dollar bill in front of an Episcopal church with Margaret Phillips to protest the church's unshared wealth, she faced her one "arrest situation." "And my husband said, before I went there, 'I won't be able to bail you out.' We lived in the county, you see, and I would be arrested in the city. So I reminded him my parents lived in the city and I could give their address and they'd bail me out. He didn't want me to go. And then the minister at this church said, when they were going to arrest me, 'You live in the county, don't you?' I told him I did, and he talked them out of arresting me. He'd seen all my kids with me and he didn't want me in jail. I didn't tell him about my parents."

For Margaret Phillips, ACTION was the logical extension of an intellectual commitment; for Gena Scott, it was an avenue for rebellion. But for Mary Ann Fitzgerald, it was a spiritual lifeboat. By the late sixties, her Catholicism was already slipping away. That her involvement with what the media invariably labeled "an extreme black militant group" cost her friends and made trouble in her marriage paled beside the satisfaction of bridging racial boundaries. "And my parents were always real supportive. Tom's weren't—they hated it—but mine were liberals, really. They believed in the Great Society, all that. But they loved watching the Veiled Prophet on TV. Every year when it was broadcast, we'd all sit around and watch from start to finish. If you started to talk, my mother was like, 'Ssh! Ssh! Do you see that gown she's wearing? Will you look at her hair?' When we'd go over to Tom's house, his family were all talking while the Veiled Prophet was on TV. I was shocked."

For all her involvement with racial protest, Mary Ann had never questioned the infallibility of the Prophet. Ruling elites "were just better than us. That was clear. They had all that money and we didn't, and there they were, on TV, at that party. They had to be better. You didn't give it any more thought than that."

I point out that the ball is now, just barely, an integrated affair. There are a handful of African American men in the society; in 1998, the first black debutante, Candace Nicole Nance, was presented.

"I wonder," I ask Mary Ann, "if that isn't a bigger victory than even Percy Green imagined. If the debutante ball is a marriage market, and a young black woman is now on that market, doesn't that mean the Veiled Prophet is approving intermarriage? Isn't that a bigger symbol even than job equity?"

"Oh, that's not what it is," sighs Mary Ann. She lights a cigarette and stares briefly at a point in the center of the living room. "I once thought," she says, "that was the answer. We'd just marry each other and all be the same color, and that would be the end of it. But they'd never allow that. They don't think of it as anything to do with marriage, any more. It's just, 'Here's my money, and you don't have it.' They won't marry their boys to those black girls."

It's a resignation I haven't heard from anyone else, and it comes on the heels of more general optimism from Mary Ann than the others have shown. At one point in our conversation I suggest that for all its evils, the ball was something people didn't want to lose because with it they might lose a fairy tale. "Oh, I could lose it," Mary Ann says. Lightly, she taps her chest. "I wouldn't feel a thing, in here."

On my way out, Mary Ann hands me two precious documents—ACTION's "Picture Magazine," published in 1970, and a collection of clippings from 1970 to 1976 entitled "Why You Must Raise Hell!"

"I couldn't bear for anything to happen to these," she says. I promise to bring them back intact in a few days. "The binding's broken already on this one," she says, touching the edge ruefully. "I'll know you didn't do that." Before I leave she shows me a family portrait of Tom and her surrounded by seven of their children and an assortment of grandchildren. She looks older in the picture than she does in person, but I don't tell her this. In the picture she looks frail and plain while her children around her beam with brains and health. In person she's expansive, unsentimentally kind. The short mousy hair in the picture looks sleek and practical in person; she's traded an ill-fitting printed dress for a turtleneck and jeans that she wears well. The one thing she misses about her faith, she says, is having a belief in an afterlife. "Tom's nine years older than I am," she says on my way out. "He'll probably die before I do. I'd like to think that I would see him again, after I die."

"You see him in your children," I offer, as one way to look at it.

"Oh, I know," she says, the sheepish atheist. She is smiling, but her eyes have grown dark. "But I want to see *him*."

❅   ❅   ❅

The next day I drive downtown to meet Percy Green at the Union Station Mall.

In the early morning, the mall is quiet; none of the shops are open. Union Station was once the largest and busiest railroad terminal in the world. Early in my life, trains still came into and departed from the station, full of commuters rushing from Kirkwood or Webster Groves to their white-collar jobs downtown. By the time I was a teenager, the city's landmark terminal was serving as a haven for narcotics dealers. The trains had gone moribund while a new cross-county highway, the Inner Belt, was under construction. This highway would lead a generation of auto commuters to new suburban office parks. There was great wringing of hands. Editorials lauded the famous architect, Theodore Link, who'd designed the train station in 1894. Old people recalled its bustle at the 1904 World's Fair. St. Louis boosters pointed out Chicago's envy of the magnificent arched ceiling.

In 1980—with heavy support from a nostalgic and guilty county—the city of St. Louis floated a bond issue. Over the next decade, stores such as Banana Republic, Au Bon Pain, and The Limited all moved into a renovated Union Station. The effort, I now hear, is failing—too many cars have been vandalized in the spanking new garage, too many stores experience shoplifting, and fewer and fewer tourists are visiting the station. But in the cool of morning, Union Station keeps up appearances. And here, along the expansive corridor, comes a well-dressed, dark-skinned man, walking with an athlete's slightly bowlegged gait. Briskly, we shake hands.

Percy Green is surprisingly well preserved, broad across the shoulders and chest, his hair thin but still black. The fleshy skin of his face shows lines of laughter and worry but not the ribbed wrinkles of old age. His teeth are thick, yellowing like my father's toward the center of the top incisors.

Over a cup of Starbucks coffee, Percy tells me first about his own father. Percy Green Sr., he says, worked thirty-five years at McDonnell Douglas and was making $1.56 an hour when Percy started working there doing electrical assembly for $1.58 an hour. That two-cent difference got Percy thinking in terms of politics. He was earning what was considered good money for a black man without a college education because he'd taken a course in electrical work.

"The other black folk," he says, "were mostly sweeping. They came in at night when the white folks left. I started asking them a lot of questions. I asked how long they'd been working at McDonnell Douglas. I asked what they wanted. And they wanted what all folks want—a better house, a good car, a good school for their kids, a good job. That's what I heard again and again. A good job."

"What did your father want?" I ask.

"He wanted me to stop asking those questions." Percy's eyes glimmer. "He wanted me to keep my head down. But I kept asking."

Soon a white worker at McDonnell invited him to a meeting of CORE, the Chicago-born Congress of Racial Equality. After a fervent boycott of St. Louis's Jefferson Bank and Trust (where blacks banked but could not get hired), local CORE meetings numbered in the hundreds. Percy began leafletting and picketing places like Southwestern Bell, where company policy prohibited the hiring of blacks above a certain skill level.

"But I was naïve, you know?" he says, blowing on his coffee. "I never thought in a million years those meetings would cost me my job. I mean, my job was in the day! It's like, if I don't like fishing, and a man who works for me likes to go fishing on the weekend, well, that's none of my business. I thought what I did was on my own time. So long as I came into work and did my job, I honestly thought I had no problem."

He did, as it turned out, have a problem: McDonnell Douglas fired him. He promptly sued the corporation. "I won," he says, "after a very long while. But I never went back."

According to the documents that I've read about his case against McDonnell Douglas, he did not actually win, though I don't press this point. I know that he managed to take the case all the way to the U.S. Supreme Court. I know the Court determined that McDonnell Douglas was within its rights to fire him because his extracurricular activities were perceived as harmful to the corporation. The Court pointed out, however, that Percy had the right to make the case that McDonnell Douglas did not fire him because of his political activity but merely to cover up racial discrimination at the company. He never pursued the case; but the decision informs cases on parity and discrimination to this day, a contribution that an easier victory might not have made.

Percy tells me that he had grown impatient with CORE's tactics. He saw dramatic events, not litigation, as the solution. Picketing and leafletting—these were worn-out gestures that were easily ignored. The trick was to embarrass the power class, to draw attention to and disrupt the status quo. The same year that Martin Luther King began to walk the streets of Birmingham, Alabama, Percy Green founded the group ACTION in St. Louis.

"It meant Action Council to Improve Opportunities for Negroes," he says. "But, you know, we changed that when the word 'Negro' became kind of an epithet. We made it Action Council to Improve Opportunities for Neighborhoods. We were always inclusive. We had, you know, fifty percent white participation."

By 1965, Percy had begun to see that St. Louis's network of political and economic power was centered on the social structure comprising the Veiled Prophet Society. "They were the same people refusing to let black folk into their party and refusing to give black folks a job. There was the same list, all right. All the big corporations. They were elitist, they were racist, and they were sexist." He pauses, making sure he's got his target right, that word *sexist* not coming easily. "They used their daughters to cement their hold."

Percy tells me that ACTION members had three goals in mind when they began disrupting the Veiled Prophet activities. First, they wanted to get the event thrown out of Kiel Auditorium, a public space maintained with public funds. The battle was over the word *public*. "Percy Green," an editorial in the *Globe-Democrat* claimed, "is a reprehensible racist. . . . Any group that leases Kiel Auditorium for an event acquires the right to control admissions. There is no basic difference in the Veiled Prophet Ball admitting people by invitation, or St. Louis University selling tickets for a basketball game."

"You know how long they used to close down that auditorium just to get ready?" Percy asks me. "Three weeks. Three weeks to hang their decorations, and nobody else can do anything in there."

I nod. I roll my eyes. I see again the yards of bunting, the chandeliers, the white carpet and the towering rhinestone-studded silver canopy on the stage, and the ornate sconces leaning out from wrapped pillars around the great hall.

"Okay, second," says Percy, ticking off the list on his well-trimmed fingers. "Call attention to the link between the social power elite and discriminatory hiring. Show the world that these very same people who party together are locking black people out of jobs. Third, call attention to racism. Let the world know that the main reason, the one final reason, why a person could not get into that auditorium was the color of his skin. Or her skin. That's why we got those admission cards, we dressed nice, we asked to be let in, and we had the reporters there when they turned us away. People said we wanted to integrate the VP. Bullshit. We wanted to bring it down. White people always think the black man wants in. We wanted to get rid of the whole thing, the elite power structure."

I ask Percy the question I keep asking, at least of those who, like me, grew up here: What does he remember of his childhood view of the Veiled Prophet, before he knew the legend lived in a context of politics and history?

"The pea shooters," Percy says.

"Beg pardon?" I say.

"Hard straws and dried peas. The stores downtown used to sell them. So you could pepper the Prophet with peas."

"Do you remember the crowds? Were they cheering?"

"They were silent," he says. He jams his finger onto the table, as if he would drill a hole with it. "Nobody said a thing. Like the way they used to watch old Nero pass by, in Rome, you know? You just let fly your peas. Next day, you knew the fat cats would have to clean 'em out of the floats."

⚅   ⚅   ⚅

After my interview with Percy Green, I wander the city. I visit the neighborhood where I grew up, now dubbed "Old Clayton," where nineteenth-century frame houses on grassy lots are being razed and replaced with McMansions framed by shrubbery. When I return to the pool house, it has been cleaned, my notes stacked, and my bed made. Next to the bed, as if for nighttime reading, lies "Why You Must Raise Hell!," the book of clippings that Mary Ann Fitzgerald has loaned me.

It is easy to dismiss the book as a period piece, with its smudged offset printing on rough newsprint, its headlines in bold sans-serif type, and its angry underlines and arrows. It includes clippings from fringe publications like the *Evening Whirl* and *St. Louis American,* as well as the *Globe-Democrat* and the *Post-Dispatch.* The cartoons in the book are by Muhammed, and the ads are from Wholesale Earrings and the Quiet Side Lounge. The motto "Learn to Identify the Enemy" dots the pages along with ACTION's logo, a kaleidoscopic swirl of black and white. The slogans are crude, the appeal

quasi-religious. In 1976, ACTION asked for a ten dollar "donation" for the big book; the suggested donation for the smaller
"Picture Magazine," was, in 1970, two dollars. A book like this in
the hands of my parents would serve as unerring proof that the
people behind the organization were crazy and violent, mostly
because the type is eccentric and the design violent. The pictures
are of young women and men in big Afros, Percy Green in a Che
Guevara beret, and plain-looking white women being arrested for
protesting.

Drinking my host's gin, I flip through the pages of the book and
the magazine. Here and there I find an anomalous photo of a Veiled
Prophet Queen, usually a girl I recognize, looking in this context
like Patricia Hearst in the prekidnap photos, a spoiled bit of white
meat. ("What did you think of us?" I asked Margaret Phillips
yesterday. Smiling gently, she refused to fix blame on the young
women involved. "We thought you were pawns," she said.)

There are some famous names in these pages—the Count Basie
Orchestra finally deciding to cancel its appearance at the 1968 ball
after protests and threats from ACTION; William Kunstler facing
John Danforth to defend an ACTION youth accused of murder;
Odetta announcing her decision to grow her hair.

The elite power structure, I think. Percy Green, at the dawn of
the millennium, is still trying to get rid of the whole thing. I am
still trying to understand it.

⌖   ⌖   ⌖

At the end of the day I meet my mother for dinner. She asks
whom I've been interviewing, and I tell her Mary Ann Fitzgerald.
I do not mention Percy Green. She wants to know why Mary Ann
got involved. I'm tired, and I know vaguely what is coming. I say,
"I think it had something to do with her having had eight children
in nine years."

"Why would that make her go after the VP?"

"I don't think she was going after the VP. I think she was getting
involved with civil rights."

"Like she has nothing better to do with eight children?"

"I think she wanted to get out of the house, get involved in something that wasn't domestic."

"So she decides to bring down the VP? That's crazy."

"I think her interests lay in job discrimination."

"She wanted a job?"

"Not for herself. Discrimination against black people."

"Is she black?"

"No."

"So she just decides to abandon her children and go mess around in other people's business, is that it?"

⚓   ⚓   ⚓

I drive back to the pool house. I cry a little. If anyone is messing around in other people's business, it is I. I check flight schedules. I call home to Connecticut and speak with my children. I call Gena Scott, who has suddenly come down with a sore throat. "I'm never ill," she tells me, rasping a little. "But the conversation we had—it's, like, opened up old poisons, or something."

"I guess you don't want to meet again, then," I say.

"But I do. I want to talk to you. Come out to my house. Can you come tomorrow?" she says.

"Sure," I say, and I mark it down on my calendar.

Thirteen

The Unveiling

He raised his veil—the maid turned slowly round,
Looked at him—shrieked—and sunk upon the ground!

— THOMAS MOORE, *Lalla Rookh*

S itting on the stage at the Veiled Prophet Ball, I was stunned
by my own ecstasy. The last brownie had kicked in. I had
done my bow. My dress was magnificent, long gloves be
damned. I loved everyone. I loved the Bengal Lancers in their red
jackets, and the heralds in their pointy shoes. I loved Lissy Hawes,
who as a Special Maid was just starting her series of bows and
looked as if she might throw up. I loved Hope Jones, former
president of the Mary Institute Athletic Association, who would
emerge in a few minutes and get her hairdo wrecked by the vise-
like crown of the Queen. I loved the Prophet, everyone's true
daddy, dressed in his brocade and gilt and wearing a gold-trimmed
miter and silvery veil. I loved all ten thousand of the elite people
who were so politely watching us smile and stumble our way up
to the stage. I loved Michael Edson. I loved my parents. I was
prodigal girl, home to eat the fatted calf and loving the taste of it.

※　※　※

I'm remembering that moment as I climb the stairs to Gena
Scott's bungalow on the northern edge of St. Louis, above the cliffs
fronting the Mississippi River. Since yesterday it has been raining,
cold, steady sheets that forced me to turn my windshield wipers to

high and coated the road with a thick plasticine skin of water. The Mississippi is swollen and brown, not far from flood stage. Gena's street twists upward among the hanging willows and heavy oaks. There is something enchanted about the setting, even in the rain, and I feel as if I'm in Oregon rather than in Missouri.

Gena's made tea. She looks pale but more beautiful than she did the other day. Inside, her house is a maze of rooms, full of hanging plants and eclectic works of art, several of which turn out to be hers. "I've been painting again," she confesses. "I dabbled in it before, but now I've been doing watercolors, and I love it."

The watercolors are all miniatures, the size of notecards, painted on fine handmade papers that fit into envelopes on which Gena has painted or drawn accompanying designs. The figures are slender—mostly women, a few men, some androgynous. One series of drawings, done in a pale-colored pencil, is frankly erotic. In some, slender, almost ghostly women hold men's erect penises; in others, men reach for women's hips, about to enter them. The delicacy of the figures saves them from being pornographic. "Sort of . . . Japanese," I say, sifting through the drawings.

"That's part of the influence," says Gena. She sits at her wooden table, watching me. I study the Pre-Raphaelite hair on the drawn women, the long Byronesque noses on the men.

"They seem happy," I say. "Almost joyous. I mean, they don't leer. Sort of like erotic angels, or something."

"Funny you should say that," says Gena, and she pulls out another stack of watercolors. "I call these my angels," she says.

The watercolor on this group is silvery, the lines Klimt-like but without all the crowding and color. The figures elongated, float on the paper.

"Jane Sauer said you were an artist," I say. "But you hadn't mentioned it."

"I'm not a professional like Jane. I gave it up. I came back to it. It's all very personal for me."

We take our tea to the kitchen table. "You've settled into this space," I say, eyeing the plants hanging from the rafters.

"I guess," says Gena. "To tell the truth, I've thought about leaving St. Louis again. I left the first time, you know, in 1973. Oh, it wasn't just the Veiled Prophet thing," she adds when I raise my eyebrows. "My marriage had broken up over politics. My sister was dying of cancer in Colorado. So I went out there for two years, to take care of her. There were other family issues. That's where my energy went. So I left St. Louis, and I left politics."

"But you came back to St. Louis," I say.

She shrugs. "It was a place to start again. But I'd closed the door on ACTION and all that. It wasn't a conscious decision. I just didn't have time for the rest of it. And people had started lying."

※　※　※

I remember sitting on the auditorium stage, feeling happy, scanning the audience for my family. My dress really wasn't so bad. My father had said nothing against it. In only a few weeks I would be penniless in Europe with the boy, Rod, who had said he was in love with me. Nixon would stop bombing Haiphong Harbor, and we would all lead happy lives. Lissy Hawes had done her bows perfectly and found her small throne below the Prophet. To her right sat the excited Bartow "Muffy" Lammert, who had slipped away in the mustardy basement and donned her Special Maid train. Now Beatrice Busch was announced, a Catholic and a Democrat, not a Mary Institute girl, but her father was Augie Busch, who made all that beer. I was prepared to love Bea Busch.

A disturbance, out of the corner of my eye.

※　※　※

"After the ball," Gena is saying over tea, "I moved back to the Central West End. My husband and I split, at the start of '73, and I found this great apartment on Laclede Place. I stripped the walls to the brick. I installed a fireplace. I was recovering. I had trouble finding work—I'd get just so far in an interview, and then the Veiled Prophet would come up. And everything would stop, right there. Then one night that February, my dog woke me up. He was barking at something outside the window. I went to the window and there was this orange glow, filling my car."

"A bomb?"

She nods. "The police put out the fire, but the car was totaled.

They never found out who did it. And there were other incidents. You know—harassing phone calls, hang ups. I unlisted my number."

"When you moved back, in the late seventies, after Colorado?"

"There was none of that. Just these interviews." She grins. "But I'm thinking I may leave again." She glances around her home, as if she is considering packing. "I may have used up my time here, you know? Done all I can. I mean, nothing has changed, has it? If anything, there are all these new millionaires. These incredible sums of money that never flow back. You begin to understand it's not about race any more. Maybe it never was about race. All along there was anti-Semitism, for instance, and there's still anti-Semitism. There are webs of power that exclude whole classes of people."

"Not just here," I point out.

"No. But here is really stagnant. Without change we die."

"Where are you thinking of moving?"

As I ask the question, I'm already missing her, this unexpected and articulate friend, with her eclectic watercolors and her memories of a time that I knew only through a scrim.

"Arizona?" she says, as if it's a guessing game.

"Dry," I say, "in Arizona."

It's raining harder. I tell Gena about my meetings with Percy Green, Mary Ann Fitzgerald, and Jane Sauer. "Jane says you came up with the idea," I say.

"We didn't know what we were doing," she says. "We were supposed to drop leaflets, really. I mean, the official line was all about 'unveiling the Prophet,' but no one knew what that meant. I just happened to spot an electrical cable. We'd left our seats and gone way up, in the balcony. The cable was attached to the ceiling of the auditorium. It ran all the way down to the stage below. I remember thinking that Percy wouldn't necessarily approve. It wasn't what he'd sent us in for. But I had to do something. I gave Jane all my leaflets. I said, 'Go around to the other side. Make noise. Cause a distraction.' I milled around until she had made it over to the opposite side and she was dropping leaflets on the balcony below. Then I grabbed hold of the cable and swung over the railing."

※　　　※　　　※

I remember watching Bea Busch. I had never been to one of the Busches' parties, but my brother had. He'd said they were held in a huge barn where they used to keep the Clydesdales, but the stalls were empty. There was a full bar at either end of the barn, he'd told me, and within ten paces of anywhere Michelob was on tap, with the barrels beneath the floor.

On the far balcony, something stirred. "Down with the Prophet!" came a woman's voice, high-pitched and echoing in the vaulted space. She was dropping paper; pamphlets. A scramble of people came up behind her. Oh my my, I thought. I remembered the letter, the one from Percy Green, it seemed like so long ago, in California. Percy Green had wanted me to be with him in the cold snow outside the hall. He had wanted my tickets.

Then, right above my head, a more serious noise—a tearing, and a shriek from the audience, and just as I twisted around, slow because of the pot, a woman came dropping out of what seemed to be the sky. Another scramble. She was hurt; no, no, she was all right. Then, she was gone, in her long dress and heels, disappearing through a stage door. Drunk, I thought.

The orchestra kept playing, the way I had heard that the *Titanic's* band played as the ship sank. The Bengal Lancers stomped the butts of their long weapons against the carpet and stood at attention. Here came Bea, up on the stage for the third bow, the one to the Prophet where she'd get her cute little tiara.

I felt myself holding on, the way you do in a dream where you're flying, the power of wakefulness arresting your buoyancy. No, no, let me dream on, let me fly higher. Only here came the woman again, the one who'd swung down from the fourth balcony behind my head and then dropped thirty feet to the floor. On she came, clutching her side. I saw her ascend the back side of the stage. I lost sight of her behind the huge oval arches and high velvet curtains that framed the Prophet's court. Then lo! Between the curtains she stepped, painfully, and with one flick of her gloved hand she did it. She pulled off the gold hat; she ripped down the silver veil.

⌗   ⌗   ⌗

"The cable didn't snap," says Gena. "It came loose from the ceiling. It wouldn't hold my weight. I'm just glad I didn't fall on people. I thought I would land in one of those lower boxes. But the way it swung, I landed on the stairs. That's what broke my ribs, the stairs. Then, I don't know—I went away for a minute."

"Blacked out, you mean," I say.

"I guess it was just a few seconds, really. When I snapped out of it, there was this man coming toward me. And I said, 'Don't touch me. I'm really hurt.' Which was honest, that was the truth. But I had to keep going. I'd gotten that far. And so I stood up and made for the stage."

I pour us more tea. Outside, the rain has let up, and the weak sunlight glistens off the wet branches of the forsythia. "I figured they took you back in the bowels of Kiel Auditorium after that, and beat you senseless or something," I say.

Gena laughs, then coughs. She is looking a little feverish. "They might have, except there was a doctor there. They did drag me back by the arms, and they were pretty rough. But he said, 'This woman's hurt,' and they laid off. They took me to the hospital instead. And later on, they'd taped the ribs, and I thought, 'I want to go home now.' So I started out from my room, and there was this very long corridor. It seemed endless to me. I started down it, and just then the elevator opened at the other end, and two men came out. They were dressed in dark suits, and I knew they were either FBI or undercover police. That's when I realized I wasn't going anywhere except to jail."

"But no one pressed charges," I say. "I looked all that up. The thing was dropped."

"Because to press charges, they would have had to release Tom K. Smith's name."

Gena sits back in her chair. A trace of old mischief curls her mouth. I have by now seen Tom K. Smith's name several times. Although newspapers suppressed it after his unveiling, they had cited him many times through the sixties, when the urban renewal propelled by his Civic Progress consortium paved the way for Pruitt-Igoe.

"But everyone got a good look at him," I said.

"Ten thousand people," said Gena, "in Kiel Auditorium. Doesn't mean the organization will reveal the identity of the Veiled Prophet."

"I remember," I say. "He was suddenly not the Prophet any more. He was just a fat bald old man. I remember I said, 'Aww.' And my date started clapping."

This was true. Michael Edson, long-haired and stoned, had been refused admission at the door because of his Semitic looks. He had asked the guard to fetch Franklin Ferriss, and my father had confirmed that Michael was my escort and should be allowed to pass. Ensconced at last in a box next to my mother, Michael had thought the flying beauty and the dramatic unveiling were all part of the show. As a stadium full of blue bloods sat in silent horror, he put his hands together to applaud.

While the Cinderella part of me watched her prophet morph into a gouty CEO, the California part of me relished Michael's lone accolade. That was my date, out there, the one who got the joke.

"Tom Smith has Alzheimer's now," I tell Gena. "His wife says he wouldn't remember a thing."

"Oh well," says Gena. "He was still vice president of Monsanto. They still wouldn't hire blacks for middle management. Forgetting the facts doesn't change them."

"I didn't say it did."

"I just wish," says Gena, "I had done something, when I was up there on the stage." Her eyes have gone moist, but it's hard to tell if she's affected by a virus or by the past. "You know, I had the veil in my hand, and everyone's attention for one moment. But I didn't have the words. I hadn't planned ahead. I don't know what I would have said. But I would like to have said something."

❊   ❊   ❊

What would she have said? What would I have heard? I remember hearing the orchestra start up again and the blood pound in my ears. No, not blood: shame. Shame, as the Debussy piece the orchestra had been playing swelled back into life and poured through me. Red-faced and sweating, Tom K. Smith shoved the hat and veil back on, crooked, and gripped his scepter.

I was ashamed that a member of my own race and sex had denuded the Prophet. I was ashamed of myself for sitting silent on the stage with the other cream puffs while someone brave and authentic took action. Most of all, I was ashamed of my moment of exultation at Michael's clapping. It was exactly like the exultation I had felt when I threw in my father's face his paltry contribution to our family's trip to Europe. I had felt shame then, too: shame for unmasking a grown man who, whatever his just deserts, craved my respect.

That was what the pageant seemed about, suddenly. Our fathers' enormous infantile need begat our enormous filial obligation. Now there was this other obligation, to justice. I was ashamed of myself because I had failed to balance those obligations.

※　　※　　※

Before I leave, Gena presses on me a watercolor that she's painted that week, expressly for me. It's entitled "Wade in the Water." In it, a quartet of wraithlike young women is about to enter a slick of grayish blue. It is inspired, she tells me, by her sense that I am beginning this book, and she is beginning her art again.

Fourteen

The Girl from Georgia

It's all so sincere.

— TV COMMENTATOR, Veiled Prophet broadcast, 1961

For many years I thought that was the end of it. The unveiled Prophet rendered both the fairy tale of the ball and the horror tale of Mokanna equally banal. Time telescopes our memory, reducing events that occurred over a period of months or years to a single point. We remember one door closing and another opening as if history had conspired to make it so. Certainly, we treat the Kennedy assassination this way. His death that day in Dallas, we imagine, opened the door to the nightmares of Vietnam and corporate greed. Likewise, the shots fired at Sarajevo brought the death of European imperialism. Likewise, Woodstock gave birth to a cultural revolution. History books may teach us the fallacy of our thinking, but they cannot restructure the teleology of our past.

This is the way it is for me: A woman unveils the Prophet, and here sits a fat old man. Pruitt-Igoe—the dream of democratic architecture, the epitome of racist housing—dissolves into $300 million worth of dust. We cease bombing Haiphong and begin, in slow motion, a rout before the North Vietnamese. A woman wins control over her reproductive system, and her choices multiply like fun house mirrors. We spend the rest of our lives figuring out which are pathways and which are refractions of the past.

My life, all of it, changed with that one gesture, Gena Scott clutching her side as she tips the hat and veil. Applause from Michael Edson, stoned. My simultaneous cry:

Yes!

No!

The rest of the night wraps up easily. The show carried on. In the *St. Louis Post-Dispatch* the next day, Gena Scott was described as having descended on "a rope" in "an exquisite floor-length light brown gown with dark brown spots all over it." "Although the incident temporarily shocked the guests," reported the paper, "they soon rallied and greeted the Queen with the traditional enthusiasm of the occasion." The orchestra "continued to play" as the bald Prophet put his veil back on and handed a scroll to the "Special Page":

> There was another trumpet call. "His Mysterious Majesty, the Veiled Prophet, in his infinite wisdom, hereby selects the fairest maiden in the City of St. Louis to reign over his court of beauty . . ." There was a grand flourish of trumpets and Miss Hope Florence Jones entered the ballroom. She curtsied left, then right, and smiled. The audience applauded. On the arm of William R. Orthwein Jr., she was escorted to the stage, where she bowed deeply and at length at the feet of the Veiled Prophet. . . . She was very tanned (from Florida) and her teeth were straight and ultra bright.

Afterward, during the Queen's Supper at the Chase Park Plaza Hotel, "few continued to play the guessing game," to find out the Prophet's identity—although, according to the paper, "the incident was so brief, and the distance between the Prophet and his subjects so vast, that only his best friends know for sure."

All the girls knew, anyhow.

"So freaking *what?*" Michael Edson kept asking. "Do you people realize we lost two more B-52s today? Do you realize we are bombing *schools?*"

"We realize that, Michael," I said.

I was, by then, on my third gin and tonic. We were in the lobby of the Chase Park Plaza, where the food was laid out. The music wafted in from three separate ballrooms. On the far right was the

Lido Room. Three months earlier, around the same time I heard from Percy Green, the Veiled Prophet Committee had requested a "casual photo" of me, and I had sent one of myself in the batik dress. This image now flashed, along with sixty-five others, like a rapid strobe light on the walls, while Sounds Unlimited played "White Rabbit" at whatever decibel level had been determined harmful.

In the center of the Khorassan Room, the Russ David Orchestra played waltzes. My mother was in there somewhere. My father had gone home early. Nancy was ill, he said. He was pale and visibly upset. Men like him huddled, now, at the tables set up in the lobby, arguing with each other and shaking their heads over their coeur du filet de boeuf.

On the left, in the Chase Club, Frankie Masters's band played a cha-cha, a dance we had learned at Fortnightly Dance Class. On the floor were the Maids of the sixties, who were now paying babysitters to watch their children while they danced at the supper with their husbands. My cousins Mimi and Carol were not there. While hitchhiking through Europe, Mimi had met a Canadian man and now lived far north. Carol, stalked several years ago by some grim reaper of the late sixties, had signed herself into a hospital, where she was found hanging by her bedsheet.

No doubt the pot and the gin were colluding in my head. But I was having these thoughts, there in the hotel. My thoughts were lighting little flames under me.

"Come on," I said to Michael. "Let's dance."

Which we did to the blaring music, though Michael was an awkward dancer—all bobbing head and loose, waving arms. People packed themselves into the Lido Room. We were hot bodies and strobing photographs of blond hair and white teeth. The bass thrummed. Then the room paled and there was breakfast, heaps of meat and eggs and sugared pastries, and Bloody Marys to sober us up. While we waited for the cab in the predawn December dark, Michael pressed me up against a wall in a side corridor. He smelled of tobacco and spicy tomato; underneath his tux he was damp with sweat. I rather liked it.

"I don't want to fuck you, you know," he said.

"I know," I said.

"I just want to fit into you for a little while."

"You mean me," I said, "or this whole scene?"

"You're out of this scene."

"Thanks," I said.

"Why don't we both go to Europe," he said, "and find Rod?"

"I don't think so," I said.

"You don't understand him the way I do."

"Michael honey," I said, and I kissed him on his soft mouth. "I don't want to understand."

※   ※   ※

In 1973, ACTION sued to prohibit the Veiled Prophet Society from using Kiel Auditorium, and the ball was held there for the last time. John Lashly, the society's attorney, who used to drive with my father to the ball, cited dwindling attendance numbers, and not the lawsuit, as the reason for abandoning Kiel. The event moved to the Khorassan Room at the Chase Park Plaza. ACTION kept up its protests, at one point spraying tear gas as the Veiled Prophet made his entrance. But membership in ACTION likewise dwindled. St. Louis continued to hemorrhage population. The parade drew only hecklers. It was revived in 1980 as the V.P. Fair and held in mid-summer by the river.

And so, say the others with whom I meet on my return journey, all is now well. All is fair, and just, and fun for everyone. "It may have been a good thing," wrote society columnist Joan Dames of the 1972 unveiling. Others declare that the great public ball would have died its own, natural death, without the pyrotechnics of Percy Green. Like slavery, I say, without the Civil War.

Exactly, they say.

※   ※   ※

I am on my way to Delmonico's, a large diner on Delmar Boulevard near Euclid. I cut over from Ladue into University City on Price Road, and I am amazed at how you can pass from one world into another just by going through a signpost. In this part of town, the small, brick houses sit close to the road: some are multi-family dwellings. I head down a middle-class stretch of Delmar through the huge pillars that mark the entrance to downtown U. City, or "The Loop." The Tivoli Theatre is still there, and the old city hall. Only a new Blockbuster building manages to account for the passage of the last twenty-five years. The road narrows through the Loop, then broadens again. Yellow banners hang from the lampposts; some carry images of African Americans that I don't recognize and those alternate with other banners on which the command "Look at it" is written. On the other side of the road, the banners have exclamation points only. The road flattens. Here and there, buildings have disappeared or been replaced by sprawling gas stations. The cars driving alongside me are now old Plymouths and Pontiacs rather than new Jeep Cherokees.

I am here to meet with the Reverend Earl Nance Jr., pastor of the Mt. Zion Baptist Church and president of the St. Louis Board of Education. Tomorrow, I am leaving town, to return to the East Coast. More than a dozen names to contact remain in my notebook. Alzheimer's has taken Tom K. Smith, who so long ago, sputtering with indignity, fumbled to replace his hat and veil before the world. "Pay no attention," I picture him saying, wildly turning the wheels and knobs of the Great Oz, "to the man behind the curtain." Joan Dames, the *Post-Dispatch*'s effusive chronicler of all things Prophet, agrees to an interview but avoids my questions by telling me how pretty I am. She uses a phrase my mother is also fond of: "*neat* gal." If you are a neat gal, you are a player; you put your energy into some charity cause. You do not make too much of yourself and are not overly bright. You usually have a hobby that you excel at, something original. A character flaw may dog the neat gal's heels; often the phrase *neat gal* is preceded by "but": "but she's a *neat* gal." If we could all be neat gals, the world would be a far better and less messy place.

I have crossed Joan Dames and Tom K. Smith off my list, but I've left the others on it. I should contact Mattie Jones, a member of ACTION who helped dress the debutantes at the ball; Tommy Robertson, who reported the unveiling for the *Post-Dispatch* but withheld Smith's identity; Pat Rice, who covered religion for the *Post-Dispatch* and knew the nuns and priests who supported ACTION; Jorge Martinez, president of the Velvet Plastic Ball, a transvestite response to the Veiled Prophet. And Hope Jones.

But I am tired. The past overwhelms me. Another trip, I think. Another time.

Reverend Nance arrives at Delmonico's with his father, the Reverend Earl Nance Sr., and three other gentlemen in dark suits, hats, and ties. They sit at a reserved table in the main part of the coffee shop, not the part under the archway that reads, "The Lord Is My Shepherd; I Shall Not Want." Within that alcove, I can see framed photos of Martin Luther King, Jackie Robinson, and other black men I don't recognize. The coffee I get is served in real crockery, with a real spoon. Breakfast is served cafeteria-style, but when we all sit at the reserved table, the owner comes over and takes my order; he seems already to know what the others want.

When I called Earl Nance Jr., I hadn't expected to be meeting with a whole contingent like this. One gentleman who was in the coffee shop before Reverend Nance arrived told me that they always meet here for prayer in the morning. I hope I'm not disturbing their session. Reverend Nance Sr. recognizes me from some newspaper photo taken when I was younger; he says he remembers me well, because I was "so pretty." Seated around the table we are: Reverend Nance Sr.; Reverend Shields, who is pastor at another Baptist church; me; a gentleman who arrives late and whose name I don't catch; Reverend Nance Jr.; and Mr. Wilson from Shreveport, Louisiana, a deacon who comes up to St. Louis for a month every January.

Once we're settled, Mr. Wilson sets out a small tape recorder and asks me to give my name and what it is that I'm working on. I figure this is the signal to start interviewing, though I'm still not sure if I'm just interviewing Reverend Nance Jr. or if everyone's taking part in this. At one point, when the food arrives, there's a break for a blessing, then we go on.

Reverend Nance has been part of the Veiled Prophet Society for five years. He wasn't the first African American to join, but only recently have invitations flowed to potential black members. He is on the committee to recruit other African Americans; for three years he was the VP's chair of minority affairs. He realizes that Percy Green and others did not want to integrate the Veiled

Prophet but to abolish it. But he sees no need to reinvent the wheel. He feels St. Louis needs some sort of large, civic-minded volunteer organization, so why not use the one you have at hand? The first African Americans in the society, he thinks, were tokens; but then those men became active rather than passive members, so naturally the character of the organization changed. He doesn't think this is just "the times"—the protests in the seventies had much to do with it, along with a general turning away from the symbol of the Veiled Prophet—a sense of revulsion at, rather than enjoyment of, the parade.

"These days," he points out, "it's not even the VP Fair. It's Fair St. Louis. No VP in there at all."

"But there have been accusations of bigotry," I say. "People claimed the bridge to East St. Louis was closed off, so fewer black people could attend. Black vendors said they were given the worst locations. They were ghettoized, so to speak."

Reverend Nance holds up a hand. "There were issues," he says, "and there were watchdogs. I mean black watchdogs, within the organization. You see what I mean? You know, if the door is open, sometimes you just have to go through it. Nothing's going to change unless someone walks through that door and starts doing things on the other side."

Now, he says, certain acts at the fair very consciously address race issues. Bill Cosby comes to entertain. Last year, the fair closed with a black act.

I ask if change can really come about this fast, especially in such a traditional community, where the ritual and symbolism of the Veiled Prophet carry so much weight. I speculate as to whether, if the heat from outside forces were to let up, the white privileged men who still control the organization would return to operating as they had before.

"Oh yes, they certainly would," said Reverend Nance. "But they are not going to have a chance to. The media, you see, and the popular reception are too much for them."

"Do you actually think," I try, "we could see a black Veiled Prophet some day?"

"I most certainly do."

At this point, Reverend Shields interrupts us. I think he's going to say something about the Veiled Prophet, or else start a prayer meeting. I've been uncomfortably aware of the others at the table, just listening to us. Instead, he introduces the gentleman who arrived late and explains that when they meet at this table they often have a guest speaker. The visitor is a representative of Primerica, a financial-services outfit. He wants to approach the council of churches that Reverend Shields and Reverend Nance lead, to see about giving informational seminars on money management. He says that Christians must start thinking about money; he says that the lack of understanding of money matters is Satan's doing. That we will glorify God better if we understand interest rates. The reverends suggest that the gentleman prepare a ten-minute presentation and come to their meeting next month. Then, turning back to me, they turn the tape recorder back on.

"Tell me about Candice," I say. This, after all, has been my purpose in meeting with Earl Nance—that his daughter, the year before, became the first African American debutante to be presented at what remains of the Veiled Prophet Ball.

"Well, I wondered about it when I joined," says Reverend Nance. "I had a daughter, and she would eventually come of age. I learned that the invitation, you know, for the girls came entirely from the fathers' status within the organization. And I have a fairly high status now, you see. So sure enough, she received an invitation."

"All there is to it," says one of the other reverends.

"What did she think?" I ask.

"Well, she was surprised. She didn't know what to think. She didn't have any of the experience, you know, of watching the thing in the streets or on TV."

"Why not?"

"Well, she grew up in Georgia," Reverend Nance says, as if this is common knowledge. "Her mother lives in Georgia."

I piece this information together, in my head.

"I believe it made a positive statement," Reverend Nance goes on, "to present her at the ball."

"And she was comfortable with it?"

"Oh, sure. She liked the other girls. She always attended integrated schools, growing up. She's at Florida A&M, now."

I am seeing why Percy Green dismissed the phenomenon of Candice Nicole Nance with a wave of his hand. She was an import, a dark-skinned token who could be whisked in and out. Nonetheless, I ask the question. "Reverend Nance," I say, "a debutante ball is a sort of marriage market, wouldn't you agree?"

He glances at his fellows; smiles. He has broken into a mild sweat, though the day outside is raw and the heat in the coffee shop low. "I suppose you could say that. In the broad sense, certainly."

"So do you think that by welcoming Candice's attendance, the Veiled Prophet group is symbolically giving its assent to the possibility of interracial marriage?"

"Well, now, that," says Reverend Nance, pulling off his glasses to wipe them, "is the real frontier. I am not saying the gentlemen of the organization realize it. But, of course, if they continue with this trend—well, that is exactly what will happen, yes."

"Yes, indeed," says Reverend Shields.

"So let me put this in context," I say. Now I am sweating too, my hands clammy on my coffee cup. "Your fellows on the Veiled Prophet board. What would they think if Candice became engaged, say, to one of the Busch boys?"

There is silence. Reverend Nance looks at his father.

"Or if you had sons," I persist. "And if one of them started dating that young woman Lele Engler, who was Queen last year—"

"Hoo!" Reverend Nance bursts out laughing. They all laugh, now that I've taken it this far. "Hoo hoo!" He takes his glasses off again, wipes his eyes. "Hoo! Hoo! The Busch boys!"

"Well?" I say. "Isn't that what we're imagining here?"

"I should say!" says Reverend Nance. "I should say not!"

"You would mind?"

"No! No! I wouldn't mind. But it would take those others a while. Yes, it would take them a while to get around that one!"

The laughter goes on a bit, then quiets.

"But I've seen it," says one of the other reverends. "I've seen very successful interracial marriages. People raise objections, sure. But if the marriage is solid—why, those complaints just vanish."

"Well, they're used to it, aren't they?" says the senior Nance. "Young people. They socialize with each other. Across races, I mean. We never did that, when we were young."

"First time there were white boys in my house," says Reverend Shields, "was when my little grandson had a sleepover party for his birthday. Invited all his friends. He didn't think anything of it."

"That is true, but." This is Mr. Wilson, from Shreveport. He's been mostly listening, up to now. "At an early age they can socialize like that, yes. But every neighborhood, every school that I have seen that becomes what they call desegregated—well, it becomes a case of what they call white flight. Or now maybe they call it urban sprawl. Whatever it is, you end up with segregation again. No different from before."

Everyone's head dips down as they take a sip of coffee to sober up.

"This discussion, here," says Reverend Nance, not ready to concede, "just shows how slow the change really is in coming. Know what I mean? Shows how much we need the structure for change. And that's what we've got in place, now, with the Veiled Prophet. Everything in place for the organization not to be racist, or sexist, or what have you. Only unless someone takes advantage of the opportunity that this new structure is presenting, nothing of substance is going to happen. It is an incremental business. And that's what I am there for. To make sure the changes move forward"— he glances at Mr. Wilson—"instead of sliding back."

"What about nostalgia?" I ask him. "What about people wanting the fairy tale back?"

"We make another fairy tale," he says with confidence. He's on the high ground now; he's wiped the sweat from his face. "That's how you move ahead."

※   ※   ※

From the pool house, I call the number Reverend Nance has given me for his daughter. She's expecting my call. "When I first learned I was going to be in the ball," she says, "I was, like, okay. I didn't know about it. But then I was excited."

"Why?" I said.

"Why, to be the first African American Maid. Making history. I was the only Maid to ride on one of the floats, in the parade."

"And the ball? Did you know anyone there?"

"Well, I brought a date I knew. I didn't know any of the other girls. But it was better than I expected. I was"—she giggles—"the first one to arrive there, at the hotel. People were very polite. I don't know if you realize, but I have blond hair."

"I just saw a black-and-white photo," I say.

"Well, I have blond hair, and I'm used to people asking questions about that. But no one asked questions. And I wore this sort of Cinderella ball dress, you know. Little straps, and tight around my chest, then puffed out. I really felt like Cinderella, at that ball."

Candice sounds very positive, very content; a neat gal. I search for a crack. I ask if she danced much, and she says no, but she doesn't care for dancing. I ask why she thinks an affair like the Veiled Prophet Ball takes place. She says it builds esteem, for young women. That coming out means introducing yourself to the adult world as someone who has grown up.

"Anything to do with marriage?" I say.

"Oh, no. It's not, like, a statement that I am a marriageable person. It's just tradition. I wore gloves that my mother wore for something, long ago. And my African American friends were very happy for me. I've always been around white people, you see. I was in honors classes in high school, in Georgia, and there were very few African Americans. No African American males at all. So I've been in the local papers, speaking out on race relations, that sort of thing. I finally came here to Florida, to a historically black college, just to get away from all those same people. But I was very comfortable in my role, there, in St. Louis. And besides—"

She falters—just barely, but I am listening hard. "Besides what?" I ask.

"Well, I never saw that much of my father. And I know this made him proud. Proud of me."

⌗　　⌗　　⌗

It is a sinking, strange feeling that I have as I pack up my bags and return my rental car to the airport. This much I know: I am writing this book because I did not answer Percy Green's call for help, so long ago. Because I have heard too many people say, "But you don't *act* like a debutante," even as their image of me changes to that of a club woman with frosted hair and a gold pin on her Peter Pan collar.

If I could tell them how, once, in St. Louis, I gave my Veiled Prophet tickets away to a gang of street guerrillas, I would do so eagerly. That sounds just like you, my East Coast and West Coast friends would say. And I'd smile and say, Yeah, those were crazy times.

But I didn't give Percy my tickets. I invited Michael Edson, who looked like Rasputin. I bought the wrong dress, I mocked my fellow debs, I ate half a pan of dope brownies that afternoon, and none of it is enough. I failed to vault from the balcony, to knock off the Prophet's veil. I sat on the stage. I sat there, as Candice Nance would later sit there, hoping to make my father proud of me. I sat there and let other people break the locks and open the doors. My rebellions were silly, my politics derivative, and my desires inarticulate. And now this young woman from Georgia is saying that she was brought in as a ringer and made to feel like a princess, and my tongue is tied in a double knot of my own making.

I like it better when people name the names they know from St. Louis. Scott Joplin, T. S. Eliot, Chuck Berry, Tennessee Williams, Kate Chopin. My grandfather knew Kate Chopin, I say. It's a good town for jazz.

Fifteen

The Queen

I don't know if this should be said or not,
but this night is an honor for my father.

— HOPE JONES, Veiled Prophet Queen, 1972

This chapter is a coda of sorts. Another question, another surprising answer.

Was there a Queen who turned left?

I know about the one who married the Italian count and killed herself. I know about the secretly married one who lost her throne. The rest seem to have gone on like my aunt Ann, marrying after their appointed year and locking the skeletons in the closet, looking forward to an obituary that notes their brief reign in Khorassan, their husband's profession, and the number of their children.

I care about these Queens. Perhaps it's because one of them was my father's sister. More likely, it's because they represent the apex of a trajectory that overlaid and shadowed my own arc up to that moment in 1972. To the extent that the burdens of privilege rested more lightly on my shoulders than on the shoulders of the Queens, I was more free to choose my path—yet with all my callow pretensions to revolutionary thinking, I had not so much as given one of my tickets to Percy Green. I want to believe that someone more tightly bound than I was also had more courage. But again and again the story remains true to form, the politics muffled or opaque.

Then I find Laura X.

I find her through a process of elimination. From 1909 to 1984, there is only one name on the list of Veiled Prophet Queens of Love and Beauty issued by the Missouri Historical Society that has not changed into a Mrs. This is Laura Rand Orthwein, Veiled Prophet Queen 1959. She is listed only as herself. "She's got another name now, though," the Mercantile librarian has told me. "I believe she goes by X."

Back on the East Coast, I dig further.

She is not hard to locate. Since 1978, Laura X has served as the director of the National Clearinghouse on Marital and Date Rape, a project of her Women's History Library in Berkeley, California. She changed her last name, according to her Web site, to symbolize the anonymity of women's history and the legal ownership of women.

I have struck gold, I think.

⌗   ⌗   ⌗

When Ms. X writes back to me, I am teaching in central New York. It is June and the humidity is high. She is delighted to have heard from me and to talk about her experience. She is coming east, in fact, with a good friend, to attend a conference in Oswego on the history of women's rights and to tour the sights around Seneca Falls. We could perhaps meet.

I respond eagerly. I offer my services, anything for an interview. A few weeks go by. Then I get a call, on a Friday afternoon, from one of Ms. X's secretaries on the West Coast.

"Laura is flying into Newark and has to get to Oswego," this young person says. "She's due in around eight tonight. Do you think you could give her a ride?"

"Newark to Oswego?" I try. "That's seven hours at least."

"Yes, we know."

"And Newark's five hours from here. I can't see how . . . I thought she was traveling with a friend?"

"That sort of fell through. She has some allergic restrictions, do you want to know about them?"

"Whoa, hold on. Not yet. Let me think."

The young woman on the other end is patient. It's still morning in Berkeley. I have commitments for that evening and for Saturday. I think about what I can cancel. I really want to speak with Laura X. If anyone has the right to pass judgment on the Veiled Prophet, I think, it is she. "I don't suppose she could rent a car?" I say.

"Laura can't drive," the young woman explains.

"Can't drive? But she lives in California!"

"She has narcolepsy. To get behind a wheel would be fatal."

"Okay, okay. There are flights from Newark to Syracuse," I try. "There may even be flights to Oswego. Do you want me to check schedules?"

"She was hoping you could pick her up. She's willing to pay you."

I want this interview; I have offered my services. But I am not a complete patsy. "I can't pick her up," I say. "It's too short notice. If she can get herself to Syracuse, I have a student. A young woman who lives in Oswego. She could be looking to earn some money. If Laura can pay, I'm sure I could talk Gloria into driving her from Syracuse to Oswego."

"She may need some driving in Oswego, too."

"Well, I don't know. I could get up there in a couple of days. Let me work on this."

I call Gloria, who is willing—even, like me, eager. She is a women's studies minor. She thinks Laura sounds fascinating. I make a couple more phone calls—checking flight schedules, fares. When I call the West Coast again, we're ready to deal.

"About Laura's allergies," the secretary says.

"I don't smoke. Gloria either."

"If you'll check our Web site and click on Laura's link, you'll find the restrictions. These must be adhered to. Gloria will have to wash with a certain soap before she picks Laura up. Her hair, too. We have a real problem with shampoos. And she'll have to de-allergenize her car."

"You mean vacuum it?"

"It's all on the Web site," says the young woman. She sounds weary and sincere. "Call if you have questions. We're here till five."

The Web site lists Laura's allergies: dust, smoke, pollen, grass, mold, perfumes, room fresheners, all detergents (including unscented), most soaps, scented makeup, suntan lotion, pesticides, herbicides, potpourri, deodorant (including unscented), synthetic fabrics, and fingernail polish. I instruct Gloria, as the Web site dictates, to vacuum her car and remove all unnecessary and possibly scented items from it, then to coat the entire interior with baking soda.

"This is starting to sound weird," says Gloria.

"I think she's rich," I say. "If she doesn't pay you well, I will."

Gloria is as dependable as day and night. Not only does she fetch Laura X from Syracuse, but she also chauffeurs her around Oswego for two days, takes dictation, photocopies several dozen pages from articles in the library, fills prescriptions from the pharmacy, and finds an herbal tea at the health food store without which Laura cannot make it through the afternoon.

By Sunday I have rearranged my schedule, left my children with their father, washed my own body and hair with the appropriate soaps, turned my car ghostly with baking soda, and driven three hours north to Oswego.

"*There* you are!" cries Laura X when I find her room—as if we were old friends and I had unaccountably disappeared at the moment of her greatest crisis.

She is, still, a beautiful woman. Her face is just heavyset enough to give character to the lines that now mark her cheeks. She wears her blond, silver-streaked hair long and loose to her waist. Broad shoulders define her carriage, and her uncinctured breasts sway without sagging. Her full lips smile girlishly at me.

Gloria shows up with more photocopies. "Thank God you're here," she says.

"Tell me it was interesting, at least."

"Interesting," she repeats. "Sure."

"Did she pay you?"

Gloria reaches inside her jeans pocket and pulls out a tight roll of very new bills. "Four hundred," she says. "Should I—"

"Keep it. She got you cheap."

❀   ❀   ❀

I drive Laura to Lake Geneva, to Seneca Falls, to Rochester, and to Ithaca. At two of the hotel lobbies we enter, Laura gasps and clutches her throat. "Someone's been smoking in here!" she cries, and heads back to the car to put her head between her legs. I get the management; they assure me there has been no smoking; we examine the exhaust systems; we set up large fans to blow the bad air out; we coax Laura out of the car. At restaurants she is even more scrupulous. The meat must be well-done and free of grease; the sauces must be made with olive oil; and the salads rerinsed and served with oil and balsamic vinegar on the side. "Generally I simply bring my own food," she says, eating heartily. "But my traveling companion had made all the food arrangements. And then she stranded me. I tell you, I value loyalty in people, and this was a disloyal act."

"Did something come up?" I ask, but Laura waves the question away. I am her traveling companion now, and I will be loyal.

We do, at last, talk about the Veiled Prophet. Laura was attending college at Vassar when, as she puts it, "Dad was selected to be the father of the Queen," and her greatest resistance to the role came in having to leave college. "I was just the wrong daughter for it," she says. "How it happened was that my father told me, in June, when I'd just come home from school. And I was barely making it there. I was way in over my head; these were highly intellectual well-trained people at Vassar and I could barely talk to them. My grade average was terrible, and I was worried about it. So when my father hit me with this news about being Queen, I was very, very upset, mostly because Vassar did not at that time ever allow you to take any time off for any reason whatsoever. My father told me that *his* father, who had died while I was in boarding school, would be very proud of me for doing this and that it was my civic duty and it would take up the academic year. Then he said, 'Well, I'll simply explain to these people that they must give you a leave.' And I'm thinking the Vassar people won't budge, but it was my only hope. I thought, 'I've got to do something to show Vassar that I really want to come back and that I'm serious about being a student.' So I went full-time to summer school at Washington University and got As and Bs. And in my free time I had to practice with Madame Kassan, with this girdle on and a bedspread for the train around my waist and carrying a five-pound something, I forget what it was, to simulate the orchid bouquet, and the scepter in the other hand, which also weighed a lot. I was trying to learn to curtsy to the floor, and to be graceful. I'm a complete klutz. I had this image of Pookie Bakewell who had to be Queen a couple of years earlier, and she was a person who was awkward, and so everyone cruelly made fun of her, but it was an honor to her father. She had no choice."

"What did you think you were accomplishing?" I ask. "What did the honor entail?"

"It was very, very clear to me," Laura says, leaning across the space between us, "that I was bowing down to a lord and master. I had recently heard that lord-and-master song, in *The King and I.* I was also profoundly affected by the movie *Roman Holiday* and the story of Princess Margaret in England—both of them stories of princesses who aren't allowed to marry the person they're in love with. And I figured I would be married off as a sort of corporate merger."

"And did you see yourself following that path?" I ask. "Or was there already a sense that you would do this and then get out? Can you take yourself back to that time?"

"I can remember the moment," says Laura. "It was what they call a defining moment, a watershed, the Continental Divide. It was that summer. There were parties, and I knew I was the Queen already. No one else knew, but they knew I was a chief contender because of my father being a prominent businessman."

Suddenly, I remember her father—William R. Orthwein Jr., with Hopie Jones on his arm, then releasing her, so that she could take her place as the Prophet's bride.

I sip my tea. We're sitting cross-legged on double beds at the hotel, PJ clad, like dorm mates.

"And there were about 750 men milling around," Laura continues, "and I could tell already that it was all about the eligible bachelors, about being sure they stayed within the flock, you know, didn't go out and marry some secretary or something. This one man, said he wanted to marry me in the middle of the dance floor. He said he wanted it because my mother threw such good parties and so he thought I could do it too, and this would be an asset to his father's chain of stores and to his corporation. He said this absolutely shamelessly, without missing a beat on the dance floor. And a guy I actually liked blew me away when I said I was going back to Vassar, he told me no one would want to marry me if I graduated from college. I knew, whatever else happened, that was the end of my marriage career. If no one wanted to marry me for who I was, there was no point being married. "

"Did you get back to Vassar?" I ask.

She sighs. "I spent three weeks there in the fall, living a lie, pretending I was to be there all year. Then I came to St. Louis and there was the ball. The ball was in October then, you know, and the parade after, and there were threats against the parade even then, so they put us in a bubble—they sort of wrapped us up in Saran Wrap or something in case people threw tomatoes at us or whatever—and we went through the streets. And this was humiliating, because emotionally I was with the people protesting. I mean, Rosa Parks was what, three or four years before? A few days later my father and I were back at Vassar, and I sat out in the hall outside the dean's office, which is like sitting outside any principal's office—you know, you're just dying. Finally, my father came out and said 'Dash it.' He told me I was a guinea pig. They were sick of this. I was the eighty-third Queen they'd had, plus one of the Special Maids who didn't want to go back to Vassar. They'd given places to us that could have gone to other girls, you know, and they were fed up. They were going to put a stop to this once and for all and were going to use me. I was not to come back ever. So then my mother went to Mr. Beasley at Mary Institute, and the story I have is that Mr. Beasley flew to Vassar on his own money and he said to them, 'You picked the wrong one. You don't get it. This woman lives for the world of ideas. She belongs at Vassar. I'm part of the Veiled Prophet organization,' he said, 'and I'll help you break the tradition, but let's not break the human being here.' So they very begrudgingly let me come back, but after I finished junior year, they suddenly told me that I would have to stay for two more years. By then it was 1961 and things were happening in the world. So I left anyway."

꘍ ꘍ ꘍

Through most of our time together, Laura X is witty, perceptive, and complicated in her opinions. She tells me about Ntozake Shange's novel *Betsey Brown,* which focuses on the events in St. Louis the same year that Laura was Queen—which was also the year that the city's schools were desegregated. She remembers defending St. Louis at Miss Hall's boarding school in Massachusetts, where the East Coast girls were surprised that her father knew how to drive a car. ("They thought there were stagecoaches in St. Louis, and Indians. This was in 1955!") She remembers trying to break barriers by visiting a Jewish country club in St. Louis County. ("They couldn't come to ours, so I went to theirs. I thought God might strike me dead for diving into a Jewish swimming pool, but I was determined. He didn't strike me dead, of course.")

Even when she compares her Veiled Prophet charity work to Princess Diana's, Laura X's sentimental pretensions hold a healthy edge of irony. "I want you to know," she says, "I turned down being presented at Versailles. And I did try to educate myself and be of some use to these charities in St. Louis. And there was Di, later, doing the same thing. In Canada she went straight to the battered women's shelters. I loved that. Though she didn't have to wear that $22,000 dress in Washington. One ought to be a little more egalitarian, I think, when one comes to America."

Laura is passionate. She is curious, devoted to her cause, and sometimes funny. She is also a Queen.

In our three days together, I notice that her allergies rapidly disappear whenever she wants badly enough to roam a certain site; and they rapidly reappear when she feels the limelight fading. In the car, she will say, "I feel a narcoleptic attack coming on," and will begin snoring within thirty seconds; at a friend's house outside Seneca Falls, she stays up talking into the wee hours. She refuses to carry a wallet because, she suggests, it fetishizes money. As a result, we spend an inordinate amount of time gathering up her credit cards whenever they tumble out of the pockets of her voluminous cotton skirt.

I leave her, finally, on a sagging porch in Ithaca, New York, where she is waiting for an old friend, a philosopher, to return and take her out to dinner. I have made it clear that I cannot stay forty-eight more hours to drive her back to the airport. "Are you sure you'll be all right?" I ask her.

"I'll be fine," she assures me. She smiles. She looks brighter and livelier than when we met, so that from within my own exhaustion I feel the satisfaction of having performed my duties well. "I like sitting here," she tells me. "You run along."

She responds graciously, I find, to a firm refusal. She is, like most Queens, resourceful. She will land on her feet, her crown intact.

That my conclusion about Laura surprises me must make me appear thickheaded. Of course, the royalty lives on, and not just in the country clubs of a faltering city in the Midwest. Whether born in the palace or self-appointed in the cell block, queens grace every walk of life. There are Marxist queens, Buddhist queens, revolutionary queens, bohemian queens, middle-class queens, and soccer-mom queens. Once crowned, forever enthroned.

⚜   ⚜   ⚜

And I, perhaps, always a maid of honor. I did not give Percy Green my tickets because I believed I owed them to my father, although I do not know, now, if I really owed them to him. I believe that he loved me—as I believe that Hugh Scott loved Phoebe, Harold Jones loved Hopie, William Orthwein loved Laura, Percy Green Sr. loved Percy Jr., and Red Ned the Wild Celt loved Margaret Phillips. That their love lay within a fixed conception of the world and what it ought to offer, and to whom, makes of their love no mean or hollow thing. It is only a love limited by the nature of the lover and the nature of the beloved.

So let us say I did not owe my father anything, but that I too, in my blinkered way, loved him.

Such is my speculation. All I knew that night—all I truly know now—is the gesture itself. The flick of the finger that can unveil. That whispers, *Now this time is over.* That lifts the latch on the gate of the future. That says, despite everything past or to come, Go.

Postscript

Six years have passed since my interviews with participants in the Prophet's unveiling took place. Minoru Yamasaki's great architectural achievement, the World Trade Center in New York City, has fallen to terrorists. The U.S. incursion into Iraq echoes Vietnam, and there is talk of overturning the landmark *Roe v. Wade* decision passed down by the Supreme Court less than a month after the 1972 Veiled Prophet Ball.

In January 2004, my parents passed away within six days of each other. My father had always boasted that he would outlive my mother, who was eleven years his junior. At the news of her demise, he seemed to let go. "Maybe I should just—" he said to my brother, and his hand made the gesture of a bird fluttering upward. He died just before midnight the day of her funeral.

Jane Sauer has moved to New Mexico; her fiber art is in many esteemed private collections and museums. Gena Scott still lives and works in St. Louis, as does Percy Green, who oversaw minority contracts under Freeman Bosley, the city's first black mayor, from 1993 to 2003. Out of favor with the current administration, he helps run a lobbying group, Jobs with Justice. Margaret Phillips still teaches classics and criminology at the University of Missouri. Mary Ann Fitzgerald died in 2003; she is survived by her husband, Tom, and their children. Laura X retired three years ago but keeps her Web site "for archival purposes" and remains a peace activist. Tom Spencer's book, *The St. Louis Veiled Prophet Celebration: Power on Parade, 1877–1995,* has been published by the University of Missouri Press, and he is a tenured professor at Northwest Missouri State University.

Its once vibrant, politically charged congregation virtually vanished, St. Stephen's Episcopal Church closed its doors in 2004. Meanwhile, recent civil rights gestures have included the appearance of the "black Wizard of Oz," Ozzie Smith, as the parade's grand marshal in 2002 and the 2004 VP Maids' group participation in a Habitat for Humanity project in one of St. Louis's blighted neighborhoods. Since Candice Nicole Nance's appearance at the Veiled Prophet Ball, the press hasn't mentioned the ball's African American maids of honor. But, according to *Post-Dispatch* columnist Jerry Berger, during the 2002 ball, "St. Louis' self-conscious elite of hairless heirs, back office bankers, personal injury lawyers, municipal judges, periodontists, corporate executives and Republican politicians" socialized "happily—if gingerly—together" with "white, black, Catholic, crasher, royal and gay" ball attendees.

About the Author

Photo by Alan Handler

Lucy Ferriss is Writer-in-Residence at Trinity College in Hartford, Connecticut, and the author of numerous books, including *Leaving the Neighborhood and Other Stories* and *Nerves of the Heart: A Novel*. She is a frequent contributor to the *New York Times* and the winner of the Mid-List Press First Series Award, the Pirate's Alley Faulkner Society Award, and a National Endowment for the Arts grant.